Geochemical Environment in Relation to Health and Disease

American Association for the
Advancement of Science Symposium
December, 1970

Edited by

Helen L. Cannon
U.S. Geological Survey, Denver, Colorado

and

Howard C. Hopps, M.D.
University of Missouri Medical School, Columbia, Missouri

**THE
GEOLOGICAL SOCIETY
OF AMERICA**

SPECIAL PAPER 140

Library of Congress Catalog Card Number 72-81723
I.S.B.N. 0-8137-2140-7

Published by
The Geological Society of America, Inc.
3300 Penrose Place
Boulder, Colorado 80301

Printed in the United States of America

The publication of this volume
is made possible through the bequest of
Richard Alexander Fullerton Penrose, Jr.

Contents

Foreword

In December of 1970, the National Research Council's Subcommittee on Geochemical Environment in Relation to Health and Disease held a Symposium: "Minor Metals of the Geochemical Environment, Health & Disease," at the Annual AAAS Meeting in Chicago. The symposium was co-sponsored by The Geological Society of America and the American Geophysical Union. Participants included scientists from many fields, and the papers contributed to a multidisciplinary appraisal and overall review of the occurrence and availability of trace elements in the environment as they affect the health of animals, including man. This volume is an account of that symposium.

Relationships between the abundance of certain trace elements and disease—for example, deficiency of iodine with goiter and cancer of the thyroid, and excess selenium with "blind staggers" and congenital anomalies—have been known for a long time and are reasonably well understood. But there are a host of other trace elements that are probably just as important in their effects on man and other animals which are unknown in their action or very poorly understood. There is urgent need for us to direct more of our attention to this important aspect of the environment.

For many trace elements, a minimal intake is required if health is to be maintained. But excessive amounts of these very same "essential" elements can produce serious disease, and this latter group of effects is of special concern. We must have detailed information as to the concentrations of trace elements that occur in rocks, waters, soils, and the factors that affect their eventual levels in plants and animals, if we are to evaluate effects from anomalous concentrations as they occur in nature and as influenced by man's activity.

Relationships between geochemical environment and health or disease in animals are very complex indeed. For example, factors that affect the availability of some elements, such as iron and manganese, may be more important than the actual quantities in the soil. With other elements, however—consider selenium—the amount present in the soil correlates directly with intake. Moreover, particular trace elements exert effects on each other biochemically, and other phenomena have their influences too, so that levels in the geochemical environment which support health or produce disease must be considered in the context of many factors and parameters.

New improved sampling methods and analytical techniques have contributed a great deal to our understanding of relationships between geochemical environment and health and disease. They are disclosing potential hazards from "new" trace metals—molybdenum and cadmium, for example. At the same time, they are providing information to show that protection may result from proper balance with other trace metals such as zinc, copper, and lithium.

Support of this symposium effort by the National Academy of Sciences, the National Science Foundation, The Geological Society of America, and the American Geophysical Union is gratefully acknowledged.

Helen L. Cannon and Howard C. Hopps

The Geological Society of America, Inc.
Special Paper 140, 1972

Ecology of Disease in Relation to Environmental Trace Elements—Particularly Iron

Howard C. Hopps
University of Missouri Medical School, Columbia, Missouri 65201

ABSTRACT

Many people are saying, this is the age of Aquarius. Many people are also saying this is the age in which we must express our concern for the biosphere or perish. Biosphere has such far-reaching connotations, however, that it is beyond the comprehension of most of us, including the great majority of those who have recently discovered it, and who so vigorously assert their willingness for deep personal involvement in efforts to save it.

With respect to human health and disease, I have found it useful to think of **ecology** at three levels of operation: (1) As it involves the biosphere. Admittedly there is an essential interrelationship among all things: everything has an effect on everything else. Unfortunately, I do not know how to formulate, much less solve, the infinite number of equations that would be required to handle this infinite number of variables. (2) As it involves macroecology, which I relate to man. In the sense that I am using it, macroecology includes those factors that have a demonstrably significant effect on man's external environment. The distinction between biosphere and macroecology (of man) is a device of communication that makes it convenient to select from the former those factors that have a more direct effect upon man and, thus, deserve priority in our concern. (3) As it involves microecology, which, as I am using the term, concentrates on those factors that affect man's internal environment.

MICROECOLOGY

Many of the papers in this symposium are mainly concerned with macroecology, focusing on the distribution and availability of several minor metals in the earth, and their incorporation into and effects upon plants and, ultimately, animals, including man. I propose to concentrate on microecology, considering the role that iron plays within man, primarily to show that relationships between apparent cause and apparent effect are very complex indeed, and that the adaptive mechanisms of human beings, which may vary greatly in their effectiveness from person to person, have an enormous influence on the level of health, whether or not disease will occur, and if so, how it will be manifest.

Although I will speak of problems that result from iron excess, iron deficiency, especially as a cause of anemia, will get much the larger share of time. One of the reasons for concentrating on anemia is that much of this symposium is about iron, and iron has an obvious relationship to anemia. Another reason for concentrating on iron deficiency anemia is because this is one of the relatively few trace or minor metal deficiency conditions that we understand even reasonably well in human beings.

Man's Dependence on Trace Elements

Reasons for our relative backwardness in understanding man's direct dependence on trace elements stem from the fact that the development of medical science was strongly influenced by a compulsion to classify, that is, diagnose disease, as a means to determine its prognosis and to provide therapy—all too often directed toward symptoms rather than causes. As a result, physicians have concentrated on the problems of disease and this has diverted them from a proper concern for health. Those biomedical scientists who deal with plants and nonhuman animals are much further advanced in their understanding of health, including the many trace elements necessary to preserve health. This concern for health, measurable and expressible in terms of yield, thrift, and so forth was developed primarily in response to economic pressures, but it is not the time to expound further on these issues. To be entirely fair about reasons for our relative lack of knowledge about man's requirements for trace elements, however, I must point out that human beings are not adaptable to the kind of controlled experiments that we can readily perform upon plants or (other) animals; furthermore, it is often quite difficult, if not impossible, to determine precisely what nutrients are included in the diet of human beings. We have collected data about iron and human health, though, largely because of the enormous effort that has gone into understanding causes and effects of anemia.

As one homespun philosopher put it—the trouble with most people is not so much that they're ignorant, but that they know so many things that aren't so. This statement is quite appropriately applied to the many persons who equate anemia with iron deficiency, and my principal objective in this paper is to point out the many varied diseases and conditions that may produce anemia as one of their manifestations, including, of course, iron deficiency.

ANEMIA

Anemia is defined as: "A reduction below normal in the number of erythrocytes per cu mm, the quantity of hemoglobin, or the volume of packed red cells per 100 ml of blood . . ." (Dorland, 24th edition). It is a clinical syndrome, not a disease. Anemia has many causes, and these causes produce their effects by a variety of different mechanisms. Ordinarily, anemia reflects an imbalance between production and destruction of red blood cells, leading to a net loss. However, if we consider anemia in its broadest sense, as representing a condition in which the total red blood cell mass is inadequate to meet the body's needs for gaseous exchange, anemia—from this functional viewpoint—may also result because of malfunctioning red blood cells, or defects in the system of circulation, or increased tissue requirements for oxygen. But, before we consider iron deficiency as a cause of anemia, let us look at the amount and distribution of iron in the normal state, and consider some aspects of iron metabolism, also some causes and effects of too much iron.

A normal adult male has approximately 50 mg of iron per kg of body weight; thus a 70-kg male contains 3.5 to 4 g of iron. Some 70 percent of this is essential for his normal cellular functions. Approximately 65 of the 70 percent is incorporated into hemoglobin and used by the red blood cells in gaseous exchange, O_2 in and CO_2 out, as these cells shuttle back and forth from the lung to the other organs and tissues of the body. Slightly less than 5 percent of the iron is incorporated into other vitally important functional systems. Myoglobin accounts for the bulk of this 5 percent, but the small amounts in various metalenzymes (four cytochromes, catalase, peroxidase, and others) are also essential for life. Approximately 30 percent of the body iron is ordinarily in storage. (This proportion may be greatly decreased in iron deficiency states.) Approximately 0.1 percent is in transport.

Although more than 20 mg of iron enters and leaves the blood plasma daily, most of this is recycled iron. Only 10 to 15 percent of the total body iron is actually lost each year. Since the normal life span of a red blood cell is 120 days, this means that approximately 0.8 percent are destroyed/replaced daily. The great majority of the (hemoglobin) iron from these destroyed red blood cells is salvaged and used in the production of new red blood cells. Assuming a normal rate of production of normal red blood cells, and no unusual loss or destruction, the body's need for "outside" iron is primarily to replace that very slight amount that is lost as a consequence of "normal" escape from the body of red cells and the (slight) inefficiency that prevents the cellular mechanisms from 100 percent conservation of iron in the course of its complex recycling process.

Iron Requirements

The chemist tends to speak of equilibrium, the biologist of balance, and I have chosen to use the latter term in the simple schema presented as Figure 1. Figure 2 is similar, but includes supplementary information. Figure 2 shows that the balance lever of production/destruction rests upon a fulcrum which, in turn, is influenced by the body's requirements for red blood cells, also the effectiveness with which the red blood cells function. Bodily requirements vary among normal individuals, which is why a 70-kg healthy male was specified in our previous account of iron content and distribution. Menstruating females, by virtue of their menstrual blood loss, require approximately 1.5 to 2 times the dietary intake of the normal adult male if they are to maintain a balance

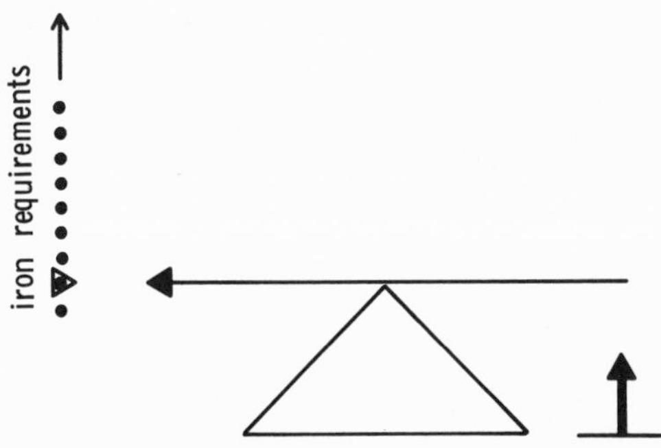

Figure 1. This simple diagram illustrates the concept that iron requirements (for Hb) reflect a balance between blood destruction, including external loss and blood formation. But there is another important consideration besides the tilt of the balance arm, the base upon which the arm rests can be pushed up.

between production and destruction (principally loss) of red blood cells. Pregnant females require 3 to 7.5 times this basic amount (for males) during the third trimester of their pregnancy. As can be seen in Figure 2, although only one mg of outside iron is required daily, ingestion of 20 ± mg is ordinarily required to meet this need because, on the average, only 5 percent or so of the iron ingested is actually absorbed. As indicated in the figure, 20 to 25 percent of the "functional" iron is derived from labile stores, and it is important that these be maintained if the body is to have reserves available to meet conditions of stress and strain.

The amount of reserve iron is regulated by a complex of homeostatic mechanisms. Loss of iron is normally limited and is ordinarily balanced by the amount of iron absorbed by the mucosa of the upper intestinal tract, particularly the duodenum. The proportion of ingested iron that is absorbed can vary from approximately 1 to 20 percent. It is this wide latitude in rate of absorption that plays a major role in maintaining iron reserves at a proper level, that is, in preserving the balance between iron absorbed and iron lost. This mechanism, "the intestinal mucosal block," has been questioned during the past few years, but recent evidence (Conrad, 1970; Crosby, 1969; Pinkerton, 1969) supports the view that it is an important control device, even though it can be overridden. Despite this handicap, it works well under usual conditions, as with many other limited homeostatic mechanisms. In simple terms, the mucosal block operates because the mucosal cell has an option: it can

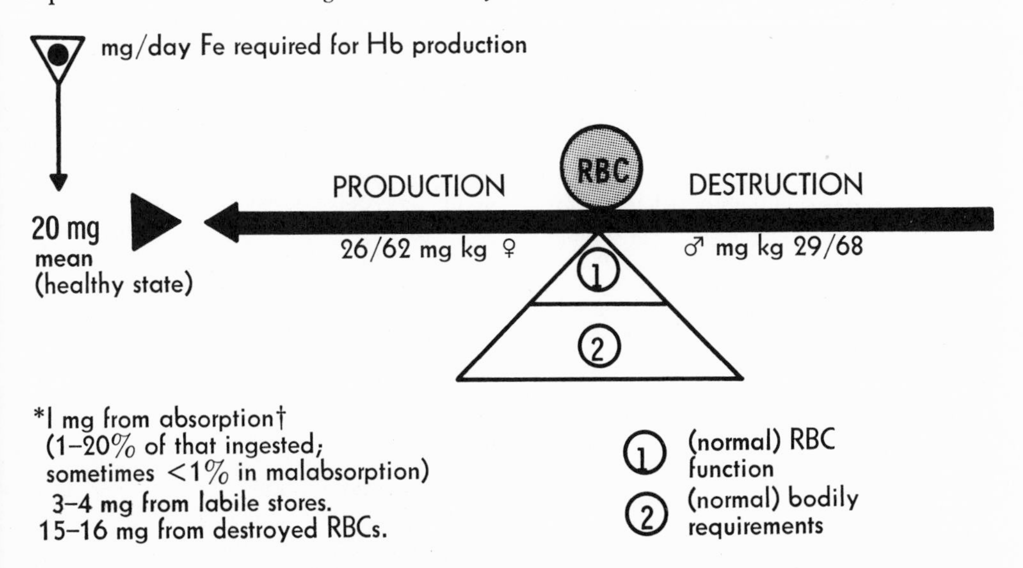

Figure 2. Additional data pertaining to the body's requirements for iron to produce hemoglobin are shown here, an elaboration upon the simple diagram of Figure 1.

retain ferritin as such or change it to ferrous-ferritin, whereupon the iron will leave the cell to enter the blood stream and make its way to the storage pool. The mucosal cells can retain only a small amount of ferritin, but there is no need to retain more since these short-lived cells slough off into the lumen of the intestinal tract after approximately a day, to be replaced by new cells. Thus, the rapid turnover of the mucosal lining is a critically important factor in operating the mucosal block to prevent overabsorption of iron. On the other hand, the duodenal mucosa can increase its rate of iron absorption severalfold, if need be. Feedback mechanisms, influenced by bodily needs, govern the absorption rate. Here again, the control mechanism can be overcome if bodily levels of iron get too low. Recent evidence has shown that iron absorption may decrease to below normal levels in conditions of severe iron deficiency (Editorial, 1968; Kimber and Weintraub, 1968). It is hypothesized that function of the mucosal cells is hampered by deficiency of Fe-metaloenzymes.

Absorption of iron is actually a much more complex process than I have indicated. Among other things, the chemical and physical form of dietary iron has a profound effect upon the amount that will be absorbed, but these factors lie in the realm of macroecology and are discussed by J. C. Fritz in another chapter.

Once the iron complexes reach the stomach, pH and Eh (though we have much to learn about the latter), together with other environmental factors within the stomach, cause many of the iron complexes to form simple inorganic salts. The presence of ascorbic acid, along with other substances, contributes to this formation. The iron salts enter the upper portion of the duodenum, and the slightly alkaline pH (it is this part of the intestinal tract into which the pancreas discharges its excretions, including considerable amounts of sodium bicarbonate) favors the conversion of reduced iron to ferrous hydroxide, the principal form in which iron can enter the intestinal cells. Then a series of cellular phenomena occur: (a) entry of the Fe into mucosal cells of the duodenum; (b_1) conjugation of the Fe with apoferritin to produce ferritin; (b_2) conversion of (varying amounts of) the ferritin to ferrous-ferritin; (c) exit of the ferrous-ferritin from the cell to enter the portal venous system. Once in the portal circulation, the iron is carried to the liver, which includes a major reticuloendothelial (RE) component of the body, and most of the iron is stored in these RE cells, at least temporarily (*see* Fig. 3).

FERRITIN AND HEMOSIDERIN

Iron is stored in the body in two principal forms: ferritin and hemosiderin. A small portion may be maintained in the intestinal mucosal cells, but the great majority is retained within cells of the reticuloendothelial system, mainly in the liver, but also in the spleen and in the bone marrow. Ferritin is the initial form in which iron is stored and, as such, is much more readily available than iron stored as hemosiderin. The conversion of ferritin to hemosiderin, which can occur quite rapidly, and the much slower conversion of hemosiderin to ferritin, represents another of the homeostatic mechanisms which, when the mucosal block is overcome, can operate to protect the individual from the damaging consequences of too much iron. An excess of iron, in the form of hemosiderin, is readily evident upon pathologic examination of the liver, and is termed hemosiderosis. As a rule, this causes little harm. Under extreme conditions, however, this protective mechanism (ferritin ⇄ hemosiderin) can also be overrun, in which case the level of hemosiderin within reticuloendothelial cells gets to such a point that it overflows and begins to accumulate in epithelial cells. At such high levels of concentration, both the reticuloendothelial elements and the epithelial cells are damaged, particularly the latter, and there occurs progressive degeneration of vital tissues and extensive progressive fibrosis that causes still further harm. We see this in its most outspoken form in the condition hemachromatosis, which disease reflects a genetic fault so

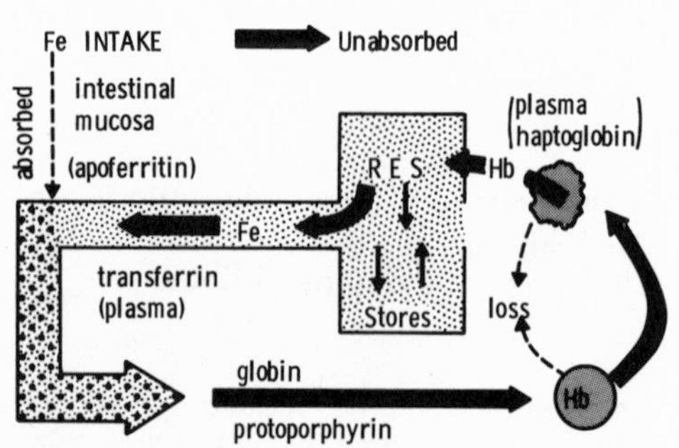

Figure 3. This simple diagram about iron metabolism shows how iron is recycled in the body, and how the relatively small amount that is lost is (ordinarily) replaced by means of dietary intake.

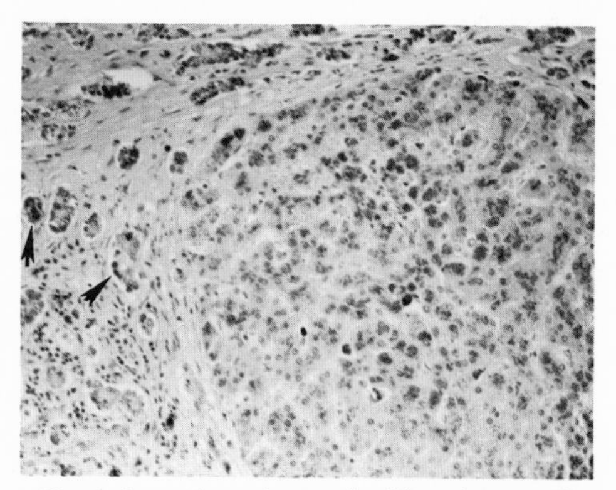

Figure 4A. Photomicrograph of liver, hematoxylin-eosin stain, 160× magnification, from a patient with hemachromatosis, showing the typically disorganized structure that characterizes cirrhosis. Note that the epithelial cells of proliferating bile ducts contain dense granules of iron (several are marked by arrows), as do also the parenchymal cells.

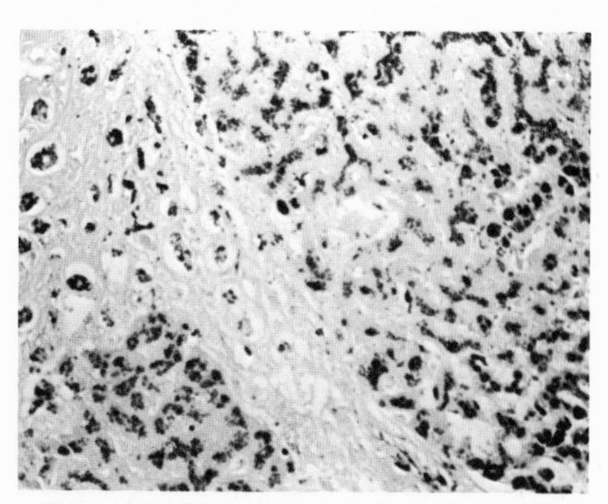

Figure 4B. Photomicrograph from the same block of tissue represented by Figure 4A, and at the same magnification; however, this is an iron stain (histochemical reaction), which provides chemical proof that the dense particulate matter shown within many of the cells of Figure 4A are, in fact, iron. In this preparation (B), the positively reacting particles stain dark blue against a pale-red background, hence the increased contrast. (I am grateful to Dr. Kamil Ishak for providing the histopathologic specimens from this case.)

that the ordinary homeostatic mechanisms for protecting the individual from iron overloading do not operate effectively, and the individual accumulates enormous amounts of iron in his body even though his dietary intake is within normal limits. Occasionally, very marked iron overloading will produce disease in a person without the genetic defect just described. When this occurs, the effects closely simulate those produced by hemachromatosis. Very rarely such a condition comes from dietary overloading (intake of several hundred times normal requirements). Much more often it is a consequence of numerous transfusions (transfusion siderosis), necessary to treat conditions such as continuing severe hemolytic anemia. Under these circumstances, the total body iron may be as great as 50 to 100 g—10 to 20 times the normal limit.

Iron content of the normal adult liver varies even more than that of the total body, depending upon dietary intake of iron as well as other factors. In the United States, levels range about 200 μ g/g; among the Bantu of South Africa, who are subject to marked dietary overloading of iron, the average is approximately 800 μ g/g (Bothwell, 1966). In hemachromatosis the level may go to 30,000 μ g/g (Ishac, 1970, written commun; *see* Figs. 4, 5, and 6).

Turning from problems that come from too much iron to those which result from too little, let us now consider iron's role in the formation and function of red blood cells. There are two principal mechanisms involved in the production of erythrocytes. If either fails, anemia results. One of these mechanisms has to do with forming the essential structures of the red blood cell, that is, its membranes and stroma; the other, with formation of hemoglobin. Table 1 lists major diseases or conditions, or both, that may interfere with each of these two mechanisms. Note that iron intake and metabolism are related primarily to hemoglobin production. In severe states of iron deficiency, tosis, which disease reflects a genetic fault so however, erythrogenesis is also affected, resulting in retarded production, as well as malformation and decreased life span of red blood cells which, unfortunately, further increase the body's need for iron.

One of the major contributing causes of anemia is increased destruction of erythrocytes (*see* Fig. 7). This can occur in two ways: (1) by actual loss from the body, as in hemorrhage from traumatic injury, a bleeding gastric ulcer, or seepage (low-grade bleeding from the gums or from the intestinal tract as a consequence of hookworm infection). Hemorrhage that occurs within body tissues or cavities also results in a considerable loss of vital red blood cell constituents, particularly iron, despite the fact that

[1] Much of the iron is transformed locally by macrophages into relatively large aggregates of hemosiderin which, because of local conditions, including poor blood supply, have little opportunity of becoming resorbed.

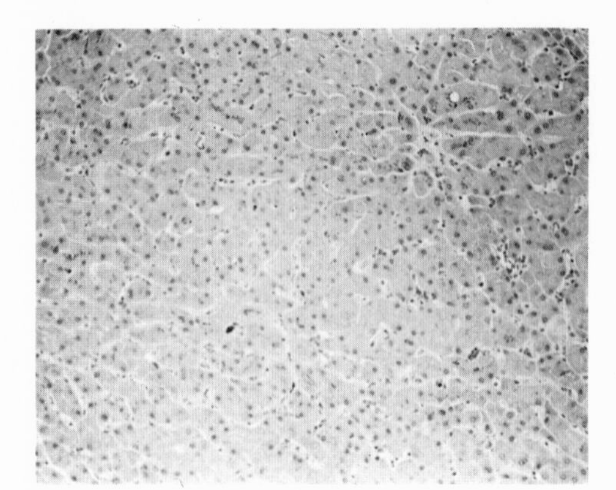

Figure 5A. Photomicrograph of liver, hematoxylin-eosin stain, 160× magnification, from a native of Addis Ababa, Ethiopia.

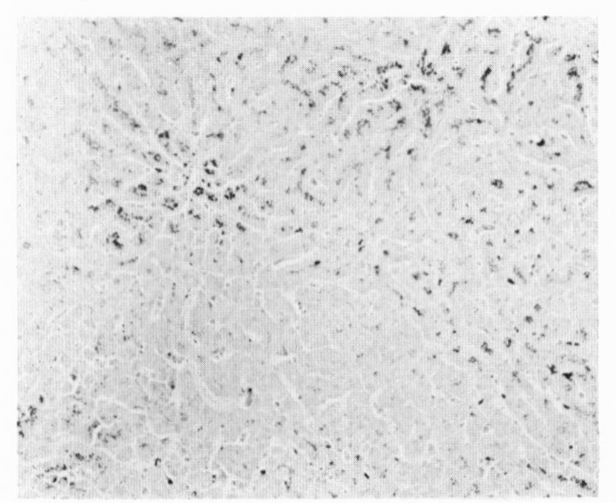

Figure 5B. This photomicrograph is from the same block of tissue represented by Figure 5A, but the tissue has been stained for iron. It and Figure 5A demonstrate moderate hemosiderosis resulting from high dietary intake of iron. In contrast to Figures 4A and 4B, the architecture of the liver is not disorganized, and the iron (hemosiderin) is not found in epithelial cells of bile ducts.

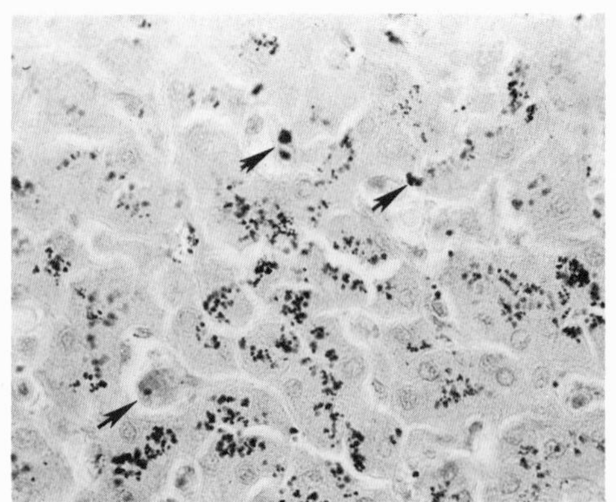

Figure 6. This photomicrograph is from the same section as 5B, but at a higher magnification—640×. It shows clearly the two types of hepatic cells that may (ordinarily) contain hemosiderin: (1) the parenchymal cells, and (2) the specialized sinisoidal lining (Kupfer) cells. Several of the latter are identified by small arrows. (I am grateful to Dr. Ronald Gillum for providing the histopathologic specimens for this case.)

there is some salvage.[1] (2) By hemolysis, dissolution (lysis) of the erythrocytes within the circulatory system. Table 2 provides supplementary information.

Hemoglobin Production

Since normal bone marrow has an enormous reserve capacity for erythrogenesis, abnormal losses (of moderate degree) can usually be made up, providing that there is an adequate amount of iron to meet the requirements for increased hemoglobin production. Often iron intake is not adequate, thus iron often becomes the limiting factor, which explains the high prevalence of iron deficiency anemia throughout the world. This is particularly true of tropical countries, where chronic parasitic diseases and bacterial infections are commonplace. But even in countries such as the United States, there are many cases of significant blood loss, and some of these are "physiological." During pregnancy, for example, unless special care is directed toward maintaining iron stores, iron deficiency anemia will probably develop, especially during the third trimester. There are several causes for this, including an increase in blood volume that, in effect, dilutes the number—and effectiveness—of the red blood cells. Pritchard (1970) described the iron deficiency anemia of pregnancy "as a result of the unrelenting drain of maternal iron to the fetus and the expansion of the maternal blood volume." The loss of blood that occurs during vaginal delivery, amounting to at least 500 ml as an average, contributes another significant drain of iron.

There are other basic causes of anemia. One of these pertains to defects inherent in the erythrocytes themselves, which prevent effective function, and several of these have been listed in Table 2.

Another of these causes (within the same general category) is related to defects in the physical-chemical structure of hemoglobin that may be either inherent (that is, the hemoglobinopathies, such as sickle cell disease) or

TABLE 1. PRODUCTION OF ERYTHROCYTES

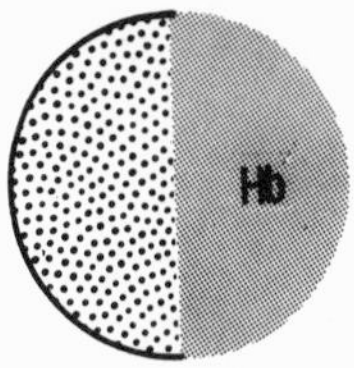

Relating to erythrogenesis

1° deficiency in marrow from:

- toxins, drugs or radiation injury (decreased erythropoietin)
- displacement of marrow cells, as by tumor, etc.

Maturation disorders involving:

- B_{12} deficiency (gastric abnormalities, malabsorption)
- folate deficiency (dietary)
- basic defects in structure, e.g., spherocytosis
- enzyme defects, e.g., G6PD deficiency

Relating to HB production

- decreased intake of Fe
- decreased absorption of Fe
- decreased transport of Fe
  - transferrin deficiency
  - transferrin block
- impaired globin synthesis, as in thalassemia or Pb poisoning
- porphyrin abnormalities, e.g., from decreased pyridoxal phosphate activity or Pb poisoning

Copper and *cobalt* are also involved in erythrogenesis and/or hemoglobin production through their effects on:

- the bone marrow — B_{12}
- the kidney — erythropoietin
- the RES — recycling of Fe
- plasma proteins — transferrin, haptoglobin

acquired. An example of the latter is the methemoglobinemia that commonly results from nitrite poisoning. As a consequence of such defects, the normal number of red blood cells is not adequate.

A second basic cause of anemia (from the functional viewpoint) is increased bodily needs for oxygen so that, once again, the normal number of erythrocytes is inadequate. One of the most common examples of this second cause is related entirely to environment, and results from living at an elevation where the partial pressure of oxygen is significantly less than at sea level.

Still a third basic cause highlights the important fact that an essential part of the O_2–CO_2 exchange (which is the erythrocytes' principal function) depends upon the red blood cells' transport of hemoglobin from various tissues to the lungs, and oxygenated hemoglobin from the lungs back to the various tissues. Thus, the circulatory system and the lungs themselves have vital roles to play. If there are defects in the arterial system that allow blood to bypass the lungs (as occurs in several types of congenital heart diseases, for example), the normal number of red blood cells and the normal amount of hemoglobin are not sufficient to meet the body's needs. Turning to the lungs, conditions that thicken those membranes involved with gas transfer, or that lead to formation of dead-air pockets, or that interfere with effective circulation through the

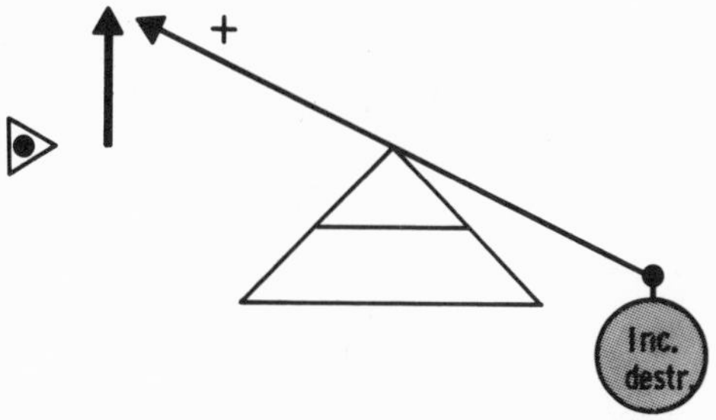

Figure 7. Requirements for increased iron, to be used in hemoglobin production, must be met if the loss from increased destruction or external loss of red blood cells is to be balanced by an accelerated production of new red blood cells.

TABLE 2. INCREASED DESTRUCTION OF ERYTHROCYTES

through *loss*, i.e., hemorrhage:

- external loss
- internal loss

through *hemolysis* because of:

- 1° defects in RBC's as a result of:
  - chemicals, toxins
  - physical agents, e.g., heat or cold
  - trauma, including DIC (disseminated intravascular coagulation)
  - hemoglobinopathies
  - deficiencies of enzymes, e.g., G6PD
  - antigen/antibody reactions involving RBC's
- 1° defects in function of RE cells (?)

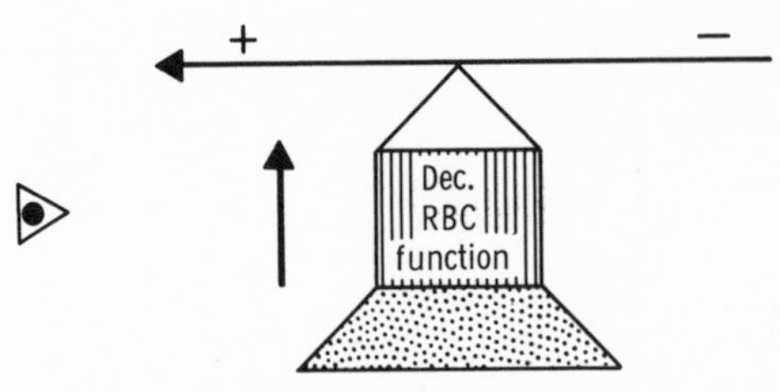

Figure 8. Although the balance arm remains horizontal, the base upon which it rests has been pushed upward because the individual erythrocytes are not functioning effectively. More of them are required to meet the body's needs, thus the requirement for iron is increased.

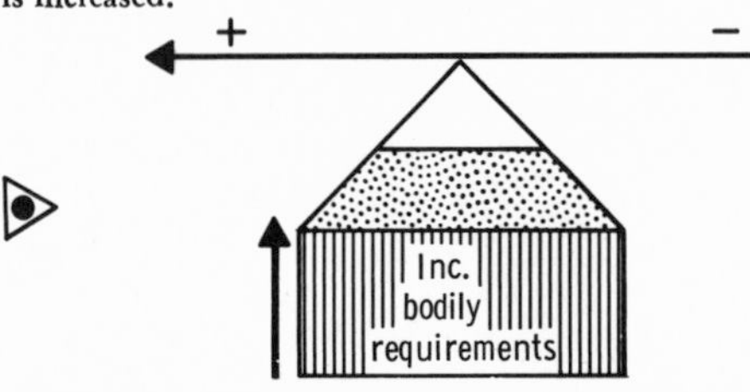

Figure 9. As in Figure 8, the balance arm is horizontal, but the fulcrum has shifted upward because of increased bodily requirements for O_2–CO_2 exchange by erythrocytes. Insofar as the need for iron to produce additional hemoglobin is concerned, this has essentially the same effect as if the balance arm were tilted in the direction of iron requirements.

capillary bed (as an example, emphysema may do all three), also require numbers of erythrocytes and amounts of hemoglobin greater than normal. Thus, from a functional viewpoint, such persons have anemia even though their blood count and hemoglobin values are within the normal range. Conditions of the sort we have been discussing push the fulcrum upward (*see* Fig. 2), moving the entire balance arm into the zone of increased iron requirements. Figures 8 and 9 concentrate upon these mechanisms and provide supplementary information.

I think you will agree with me that direct and simple connections between deficiency of iron and the particular disease manifestation we have focused upon, anemia, are far more apparent than real. The same can be said for deficiency of almost any other trace or microelement and its effects on health.

Other papers from this conference will provide many more illustrations of complex interrelationships between individual trace and microelements, and health and disease. We must recognize the complexity of such connections if we are to have an effective understanding of how causes and effects are associated with each other. And we must understand these associations if we are to preserve health, or, as the occasion warrants, cure disease.

REFERENCES CITED

Bothwell, T. H., 1966, The diagnosis of iron deficiency; New Zealand Med. J. Suppl., 65:880.

Conrad, M. E., 1970, Factors effecting the absorption of iron, *in* Hallberg, L., Harwerth, H.-G., and Vannotti, A., eds., Iron deficiency: New York, Academic Press, 628 p.

Crosby, W. H., 1969, Intestinal response to the body's requirement for iron: Am. Med. Assoc. Jour., v. 208, p. 347–351.

Pinkerton, P. H., 1969, Control of iron absorption by the intestinal epithelial cell—review and hypothesis: Annals. Intern. Med., v. 70, p. 401–408.

Editorial, 1968, Tired cells: New England Jour. Med., v. 279, p. 488–489.

Kimber, C., and Weintraub, L. R., 1968, Malabsorption of iron secondary to iron deficiency: New England Jour. Med., v. 279, p. 453–459, 1968.

Pritchard, J. A., 1970, Anemias complicating pregnancy and the puerperium, Chapter 4, *in* (Committee on Maternal Nutrition/Food and Nutrition Board/National Research Council), Maternal nutrition and the course of pregnancy: Washington, D.C., Natl. Acad. Sci., 241 p.

Manuscript Received by the Society September 27, 1971

Published in The Geological Society of America Bulletin, March, 1972.

PRINTED IN U.S.A.

The Geological Society of America, Inc.
Special Paper 140, 1972

Trace Elements in Soils and Factors That Affect Their Availability

Robert L. Mitchell
Macaulay Institute for Soil Research, Aberdeen, Scotland

ABSTRACT

Plants are dependent on the local soil, and the intake of farm animals can be regulated, but man draws his food, and so his trace elements, from the most convenient source. Nevertheless, soil is ultimately the primary natural source of trace elements in animals and man. The factors that control their levels in different soils, their availability to plants, and their contents in different plant species are discussed from the point of view of the amounts available to animals and man.

GEOCHEMICAL ENVIRONMENT

In the establishment of the relationship of the geochemical environment to health and disease in a developed society, the significance of the local soil is possibly less than might appear at first sight. The soil-plant-animal system which provides the bulk of human food is illustrated diagramatically, in vastly simplified form, in Figure 1. The crop-plant is fixed on its own particular soil, and the farm animal is generally captive, but man is free to draw his food from the most convenient source, which is seldom his own immediate environment. In an industrial community probably the only constant factors applicable to the whole population are the air man breathes and the piped water he drinks. Only in a closed or primitive community, where contributions from outside the environmental circle are essentially absent, can a good correlation between soil and health reasonably be anticipated, provided there is some constancy of soil type over the area of community activity, and there are no major differences between groups within the community in respect of the proportions of different plant or animal products in their diets.

Despite these reservations regarding direct environmental correlation, soil is, in fact, the primary natural source of most trace elements in plants and animals and, through them, in man. It is, therefore, essential to appreciate the factors that control trace element content and availability in soils.

TOTAL TRACE-ELEMENT CONTENT

A soil is formed from a parent material derived from rock, but not necessarily the underlying rock. Often the soil parent material is a surface deposit of fluvial, marine, glacial, or aeolian origin whose nature at any location has to be established by the soil surveyor. In such circumstances the parent rock should be shown to originate outside rather than within the environmental enclave in Figure 1.

When the nature of the parent material of a young soil is known, it is possible to assess the probable total contents of the different trace elements. Such conditions apply in Scotland, where 12,000 yrs ago the whole area was ice covered, and the present soils have developed on a layer of mechanically comminuted boulder clay derived from the rocks over which the ice had passed. This drift is not necessarily wholly or even partially composed of the underlying rock, but may have been transported several miles; furthermore, the geology of Scotland is so complex that major changes in the overlying boulder clay can occur within distances of a few yards. Soils developed on this

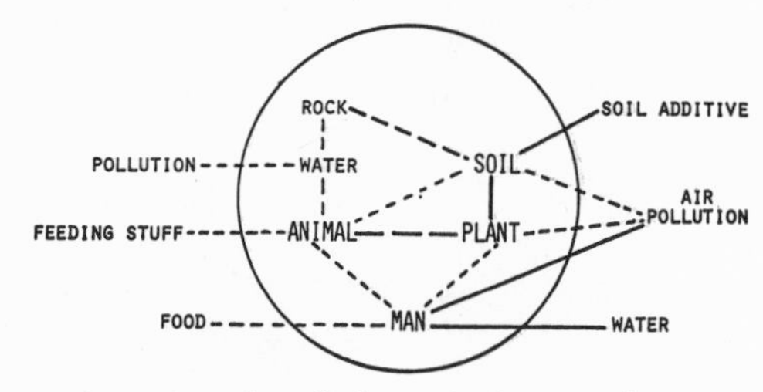

Figure 1. The soil-plant-animal system illustrating the sources of nutrient supply from within and without the immediate environmental circle.

type of material are useful in the study of trace-element behavior, but are much too variable in composition for the establishment of regional differences affecting health or disease in plant, animal, or man. Fortunately, a large proportion of the agricultural soils of Scotland have been surveyed systematically and the nature of their parent materials established, so that their trace element status can be predicted fairly accurately. The principles controlling the trace-element contents in these agricultural soils have been reviewed and reported (Mitchell, 1964). In Table 1 some of the more interesting variations are illustrated. We expect to find relatively high contents of cobalt, nickel, and chromium in young soils derived from ultrabasic rocks, intermediate amounts from basic rocks, and low contents of these elements in transitional and acid rocks. On the other hand, elements such as rubidium reach their highest contents in the more silica-rich igneous rocks. The range of content of biologically important elements such as manganese, zinc, copper, and molybdenum in the commoner igneous rocks is not so wide, being of the order of 10-fold rather than 100–1000 fold, with less marked differentiation trends.

In the course of geological weathering, most of the biologically important trace metals in igneous rocks find a place in argillaceous sediments, whose normal content is near the average content of igneous rocks. In some instances, however, there may be selective concentration of some elements, notably molybdenum and selenium. Arenaceous and calcareous rocks tend to be low in biologically interesting elements.

TABLE 1. TOTAL TRACE-ELEMENT CONTENT OF TYPICAL SCOTTISH ARABLE SURFACE SOILS DEVELOPED ON GLACIAL TILL DERIVED FROM DIFFERENT ROCK TYPES (PPM IN DRY MATTER)

	Serpentine	Olivine gabbro	Andesite	Trachyte	Granite
Co	80	40	8	4	<2
Ni	800	50	10	25	10
Cr	3,000	300	60	60	5
Mo	1	2	<1	3	<1
Cu	20	40	10	<10	<10
Mn	3,000	5,000	800	1,500	700
Rb	60	70	30	250	600

	Granitic gneiss	Quartz mica schist	Shale	Sand-stone	Quartzite
Co	10	25	20	<3	20
Ni	40	80	40	15	50
Cr	200	150	200	30	250
Mo	<1	5	<1	<1	1
Cu	25	100	10	<10	40
Mn	1,000	3,000	1,000	200	1,000
Rb	500	200	250	<30	300

Alterations that arise as a result of metamorphism of sedimentary rocks tend to change the mode of occurrence rather than the amount of the trace elements. These trends are also illustrated in Table 1; information on other elements has been presented in Mitchell (1964). The quartzitic soil has developed on boulder clay, which has obviously been contaminated by material from an adjoining ultrabasic rock.

The total content of a trace element in a soil, especially a young mineral soil, gives little information on the amount that is likely to be present in a form capable of being taken up by plants. It is largely bound up in the crystal lattice of the constituent minerals of the parent material. When abnormally high or low, it can indicate the possibility of absolute excess or deficiency, but generally, the total content in a soil is of little diagnostic use. It is the extent to which a trace element has been mobilized and stored in the soil in an available form that is significant.

It must be pointed out that the more mature a soil, particularly under conditions that encourage pedological weathering such as high temperature and high rainfall, the less the influence of soil parent material on the chemical composition of the soil; this applies not only to the major constituents, but also to individual trace elements. Their total content in the resultant soil may increase or decrease depending on their chemical properties and modes of occurrence and on the nature of the weathering process. Soils which have been under development for hundreds of thousands of years may reflect the effects of several pedological cycles and have a composition which bears little relationship to that of the parent rock. Different rocks may produce similar soils. Behavior of trace-elements illustrated in this paper is that operative under moist temperate conditions: the emphasis should be somewhat different for tropical soils, although the principles are similar.

MOBILIZATION OF TRACE ELEMENTS

The factors controlling the location of trace elements in the unweathered minerals of igneous rocks are summarized in Mitchell (1964). Essential elements, such as copper, manganese, zinc, cobalt and molybdenum, as well as vanadium and such possibly toxic elements as nickel and lead are largely accommodated in the readily weathered minerals, particularly ferromagnesian minerals, such as olivine, hornblende, augite, and biotite, and only exceptionally in their own oxide or sulphide minerals. As a result of pedological weathering they gradually become mobilized and thereby accessible to plants. The rate of mobilization often corresponds roughly to the requirements of the vegetation that develops naturally on the soil. In some sedimentary rocks the situation regarding mobilization may be rather less favorable, as the secondary minerals in which the trace elements may occur are at the end of the weathering chain and tend to be stable under the conditions prevailing in freely drained soils.

The forms in which mobilized trace elements are held in soils for uptake by plants include: (1) in solution in ionic or combined form, in which case they can be removed from the soil by water extraction; (2) as readily exchangeable ions in inorganic or organic exchange-active complexes, extractable by neutral salts such as ammonium acetate; (3) as more firmly bound ions in the exchange complexes, extractable by dilute acetic acid or a chelating agent such as EDTA; (4) in insoluble organic or organo-mineral complexes, extractable by EDTA; (5) incorporated in precipitated oxides or other insoluble salts, extractable by vigorous extractants such as acid ammonium oxalate; (6) in secondary minerals in a fixed form.

The proportion of a trace element present in any one form depends on the nature and amount of the clay minerals and organic matter and on the pH and Eh of the soil, as well as on the properties of the element in question.

For instance, when copper is released during weathering, it is quickly chelated by organic complexes in the soil and, in acid mineral soils, held in a form that is largely available to plants. It has been shown (Hodgson and others, 1966) that in some mineral soils over 90 percent of the soluble copper is present in organic combination compared with <75 percent of the zinc. The stability of metal chelates in the soil depends, among other factors, on the soil pH and the nature of the chelate. Cobalt, on the other hand, appears to be present largely as firmly bound but still exchangeable ions in the exchange complex. In some soils, however, cobalt may be rapidly removed from the soil solution by oxides of manganese and in due course fixed in an unavailable form.

The lower horizons of freely drained soils show little mobilization of trace elements, although in the surface horizon of arable soils there is generally sufficient weathering to meet plant requirements. In adjacent poorly drained or gleyed soils on the same parent material, the ferromagnesian and other less stable minerals undergo considerable weathering, and a significant proportion of some trace elements is mobilized even at some depth. The effects in adjoining freely drained and very poorly drained soils on an olivine gabbro boulder clay are demonstrated for cobalt and copper in Figures 2 and 3 (Berrow, 1958). The parent materials contained about 30 ppm cobalt and 20 ppm copper, so that quite a substantial proportion of the total content is mobilized to a considerable depth in the poorly drained soil. The practical effect is illustrated in Table 2 (*from* Mitchell and others, 1957a) for the uptake of cobalt, nickel, molybdenum and copper by clover and rye grass from freely drained and poorly drained soils derived from an argillaceous schist. The increase in uptake resulting from the effects of impeded drainage varies from almost tenfold for cobalt to <25 percent for copper (in clover only), although in each case the extractable levels in the soils varied by threefold.

SOIL-PLANT TRANSFER

The plant root draws its supply of nutrients from the soil zone in its immediate neighborhood. Several processes are involved in the

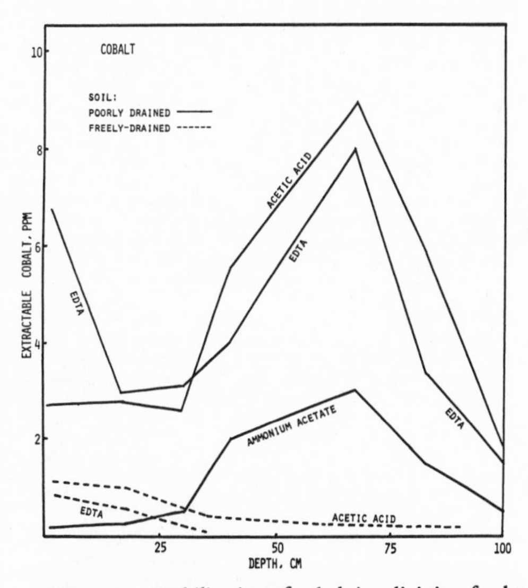

Figure 2. Mobilization of cobalt in adjoining freely drained and poorly drained soil profiles developed on similar parent materials derived from olivine gabbro, demonstrated by extraction with normal ammonium acetate, 2.5 percent acetic acid, and 0.05 molar EDTA.

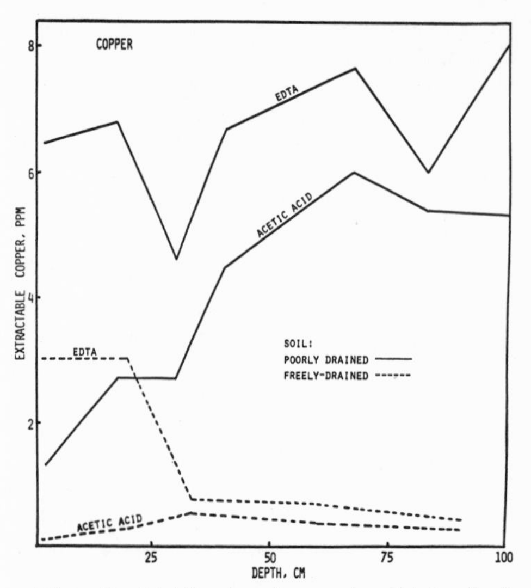

Figure 3. Mobilization of copper in adjoining freely drained and poorly drained soil profiles developed in similar parent materials derived from olivine gabbro and demonstrated by extraction with normal ammonium acetate, 2.5 percent acetic acid, and 0.05 molar EDTA.

TABLE 2. EFFECT OF PEDOLOGICAL DRAINAGE CONDITIONS ON TRACE-ELEMENT MOBILIZATION AND PLANT UPTAKE*

	Cobalt		Nickel		Molybdenum		Copper	
Drainage	Free	Poor	Free	Poor	Free	Poor	Free	Poor
Soil extractable	1.3†	2.9†	1.3†	3.4†	0.06§	0.19§	2.6§	6.6§
Red clover	0.16	1.4	2.0	5.9	1.0	3.1	7.9	10.3
Rye grass	0.18	1.5	1.0	3.4	0.7	1.2	4.0	3.4

* *Contents in surface soils and plants from freely and poorly drained portions of the same field on the same soil parent material (ppm in dry matter). From Mitchell and others (1957a).*

† *Soluble in acetic acid.*

§ *Extractable by EDTA.*

repletion of this zone once it has been depleted by plant uptake. These are illustrated diagrammatically in Figure 4 which attempts to show the steps involved between the weathering of minerals or decomposition of organic residues and uptake by the plant.

Nye (1967) and Graham-Bryce (1967) and most workers agree that the two most important factors are mass flow of the soil solution to replace the liquid directly absorbed into the

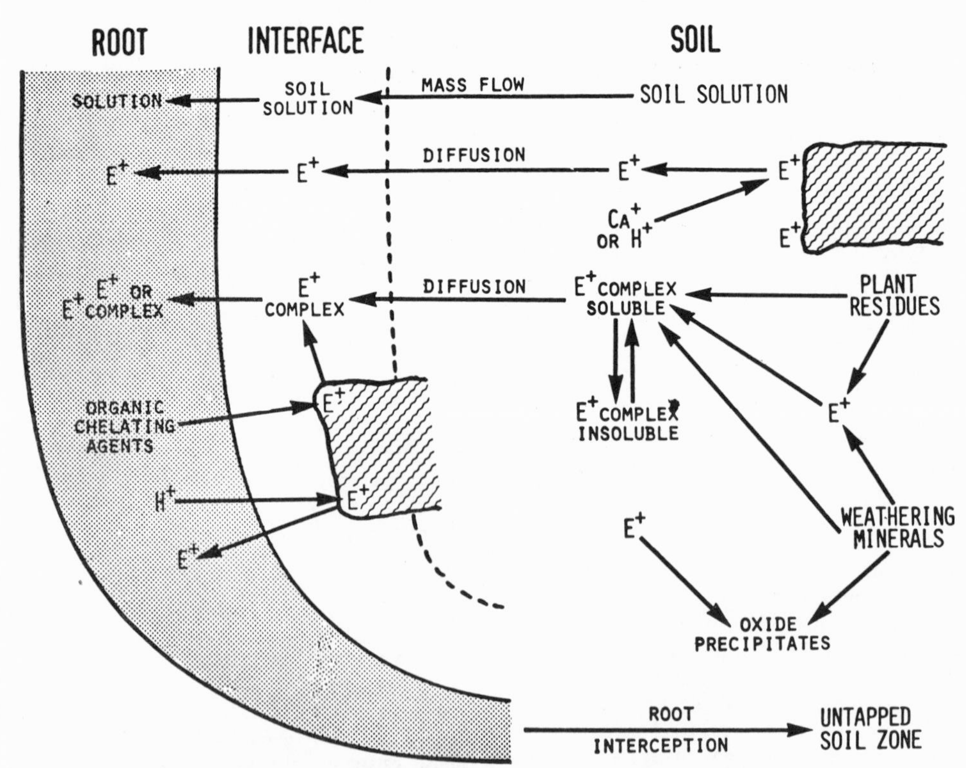

Figure 4. The principal processes operative in the transfer of trace elements from the soil to the plant root. The general symbol E^+ is used to represent any trace-element cation that can participate in the particular process illustrated. A complementary diagram could be produced to illustrate anionic processes.

root and diffusion of constituents of the soil solution toward the root zone down the concentration gradient created by the absorption of ions, salts, or other constituents of the solution into the root. Opinions differ regarding the significance of root interception: Oliver and Barber (1966) postulate that the root develops and penetrates into untapped areas, as a result of local nutrient depletion.

These processes could account for the uptake of many of the major nutrients and some of the trace elements, for instance, manganese and molybdenum (Barber and others, 1967). For other trace elements this hypothesis would necessitate a degree of mobility in the soil solution that may not exist. Because of the firmness with which they are held in the adsorbing complex, it would seem that for many trace elements some process involving transfer from the more firmly bound state may take place, possibly in the immediate root zone where there are increased concentrations of hydrogen ions and organic chelating agents exuded by the roots or rhizosphere organisms. Hodgson and others (1967) consider that soluble complexing agents, such as those known to be secreted by roots, "are potentially an important factor in increasing the transport of certain ions to roots." At which point in the course of uptake a breakdown of such complexes takes place has not been definitely established.

As already indicated, the most available form in which an element occurs in a soil depends on its chemical properties and the nature of the possible binding agents. In acid mineral soils, some elements, such as boron, occur largely as an oxy-acid in the soil solution; the alkalis and alkaline earths are present as readily exchangeable cations, and some metals, including cobalt, nickel, zinc, and lead occur as more firmly bound exchangeable cations. Copper, and to some extent zinc, are held in organic or mineral-organic complexes, and other elements such as manganese are present as relatively insoluble oxides or other compounds whereas available molybdenum is present largely as weakly adsorbed anion. In soils rich in organic matter organic combination must play a greater role.

It is obvious, when assessing availability, that an extractant providing only a single value determination of one or more of the forms in which a trace element may occur cannot make allowance for all the variables involved (discussed *by* Williams, 1962). Such determinations give a rather arbitrary measurement of a "quantity factor," without providing information regarding the "intensity factor" related to the binding power of the soil, or regarding a "rate factor" involving the mobilization process. Methods of assessment taking these aspects into account are being developed by various workers.

In carrying out experiments to measure trace-element uptake by plants, the difference in behavior between solution culture and soil culture must be appreciated. Copper cations, for instance, can occur in the former, but are essentially absent from the latter, because they are rapidly removed from the soil solution by chelating agents or exchange-active sites. Nevertheless, solution culture serves a useful purpose in the investigation of soil-plant relations. It has been shown (DeKock and Mitchell, 1957) that divalent zinc, copper, or nickel in ionic form is accepted into mustard or tomato leaves five to ten times more effectively than the EDTA chelate. On the other hand, trivalent metals pass into the leaf more readily when present as chelate, without injuring the plant, as do the trivalent cations. The results for gallium in Table 3 show that when toxicity occurs, the gallium ions are concentrated at the root; when the metal is complexed, it passes innocuously into the plant. The possible effect on an animal consuming such plants is another matter possibly because of an effect such as this. Some soils near Aberdeen carry plants with titanium contents up to ten times the normal level.

MODIFICATION OF THE TRACE ELEMENT STATUS OF SOILS

In many instances the simplest means of increasing trace-element uptake by plants is to add the trace element to the soil in an appropriate form. This is illustrated by the addition of cobalt to deficient Scottish soils, in which its effect persists over at least four years when added as sulphate, but is scarcely obvious in the second year when added as an organic chelate. Clover and rye grass behave somewhat similarly regarding cobalt uptake and persistence, as indicated in Figure 5, which is based largely on the results quoted by Reith and Mitchell (1964). On some South Australian

TABLE 3. EFFECT OF CHELATION ON Ga UPTAKE AND GROWTH OF MUSTARD IN SOLUTION CULTURE*

	Root	Stem	Leaf	Plant height	Appearance
Ga^{+++}	2,000	0.9	0.5	11 cm	Severely chlorotic
Ga EDTA	100	34	67	23 cm	Dark green

* *Ga present at 2 ppm as $Ga(NO_3)_3$ or Ga EDTA (ppm in dry matter).*

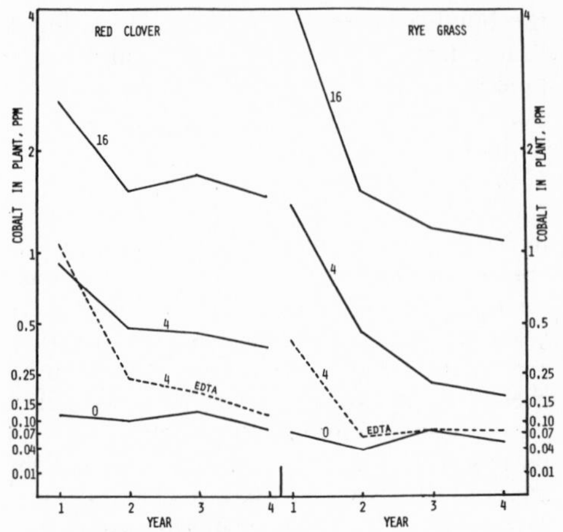

Figure 5. The effect of one addition of cobalt to the soil on the uptake by red clover and rye grass, for four years after its application as cobalt sulphate or cobalt EDTA chelate at the rates indicated in pounds per acre.

soils, added cobalt becomes unavailable after a few months: in these soils most of the cobalt is associated with manganese in the minerals birnessite and lithiophorite, and Taylor and McKenzie (1966) suggest a specific scavenging effect of these minerals for cobalt. Similar selective immobilizing effects must be anticipated for other trace elements. Manganese added to a soil seldom remains available, except in very acid conditions.

Figure 6. The relation between the copper content of red clover or rye grass and the EDTA-extractable copper in the soil.

An increase in soil content may not affect all plant species similarly. When the available copper in a soil increases, the content in clover growing on that soil rises, while the content in grasses in the same mixed herbage remains relatively constant, as shown in Figure 6, which is based largely on results quoted by Mitchell and others (1957b). Copper deficient soils, therefore, can be diagnosed by analyzing clover, but not the grasses that accompany it in a mixed herbage, although it is the yield of cereals and similar monocots that suffers from a copper deficiency in soil.

Plant uptake can also be substantially modified for some elements by changes in soil pH of the order brought about by normal agricultural liming operations. The elements most affected are cobalt, nickel, zinc, manganese and molybdenum. As seen in Table 4, from Mitchell (1951), a rise in the pH of a granitic soil from 5.4 to 6.4 following liming reduces the uptake by red clover of cobalt, nickel, and manganese by one-half, while that of molybdenum is increased sixfold. A reduction in zinc uptake is frequently observed on other soils. There is some evidence that soil pH affects most markedly the uptake of trace elements present in ionic form or as partially soluble salts: uptake of molybdenum from organic-rich soils may be high at a pH 5 or below, and not significantly increased by liming.

The application of certain fertilizers can induce trace-element deficiency. It would appear that regular additions of nitrogen to some soils can bring about copper deficiency in cereals, while overgenerous application of phosphate may give rise to zinc deficiency.

Environmental pollution cannot be excluded. In some urban areas in Scotland the soils of parklands and gardens have, in addition to lead, the best known atmospheric contaminant, contents of extractable copper, zinc, and boron from five to ten times as high as in corresponding rural soils (Purves, 1968). These are probably derived from smoke and soot originating from the bituminous coal fires used in Scottish cities during the past two centuries. A parallel effect can arise in garden soils in coun-

TABLE 4. EFFECT OF LIMING ON THE UPTAKE OF TRACE ELEMENTS BY RED CLOVER FROM A GRANITIC SOIL (PPM IN DRY MATTER)

Soil pH	Co	Ni	Mo	Zn	Cu	Mn
5.4	0.26	2.02	0.31	61	12.5	56
6.1	0.20	1.40	1.60	44	14.0	42
6.4	0.16	1.04	1.78	51	13.0	25

TABLE 5. UPTAKE OF TRACE ELEMENTS BY DIFFERENT CONSTITUENT SPECIES OF A MIXED HERBAGE (PPM IN DRY MATTER)

	Mo	Mn	Mn/Mo
Clover	7.3	86	12
Cocksfoot	1.3	142	109
Crested dogstail	0.5	114	228

try districts if soot, flue dusts, or ashes are added to the soil. This is important in the attempt to correlate soils diagnostically with human health: the person who attempts to exist almost entirely off his own small piece of land is the one most likely to have modified it substantially by various forms of treatment. The use of some sewage sludges from urban industrial areas may be particularly undesirable, as excessive amounts of toxic trace elements may be present, as confirmed by Berrow and Webber (1972).

ASSESSMENT OF AVAILABILITY BY PLANT UPTAKE

When an attempt is made to correlate soil status directly with animal or human disorders, account is seldom taken of how much the plant content of an element can vary from species to species, with the stage of growth and within the different parts of a plant. Root to above-ground differentiation has already received comment (Table 3). The species effect is illustrated in Table 5 for three constituents of a mixed herbage, extracted from more comprehensive results quoted by Reith and Mitchell (1964). Such species relationship for a particular element is not constant, but can vary with the soil content, as pointed out for the rye-grass:red-clover ratio in Figure 5 illustrating the uptake of copper. No practical significance is ascribed to the Mn/Mo ratio: it is quoted solely to illustrate the varying behavior of different elements.

An instance of unusual uptake of cobalt by cocksfoot is difficult to explain (Table 6; Mitchell and others, 1957a). The individual species in soils A, B, and C behave as expected for cobalt deficient, cobalt adequate, and marginal soils, respectively, but the cobalt content of cocksfoot from soil D, adjacent to soil C, and derived from the same granitic gneiss, is exceptional, and some undiagnosed factor must be involved. The seasonal effect is illustrated for cobalt and manganese in Table 7, where the Mn/Co ratio varies in cocksfoot, but remains constant in rye grass, despite large changes in absolute amount.

TABLE 6. UPTAKE OF COBALT BY CONSTITUENT SPECIES OF A MIXED HERBAGE ON SOILS A, B, C, D (PPM IN DRY MATTER)

	A	B	C	D
Mixed herbage	0.04	0.17	0.10	0.26
Clover	0.08	0.35	0.19	0.18
Rye grass	0.04	0.11	0.08	0.06
Cocksfoot	0.03	0.12	0.09	0.36

TABLE 7. VARIATION IN TRACE-ELEMENT UPTAKE BY TWO SPECIES IN A MIXED HERBAGE AT DIFFERENT DATES OF SAMPLING (PPM IN DRY MATTER)

Date	Cocksfoot			Rye grass		
	Co	Mn	Mn/Co	Co	Mn	Mn/Co
June 13	0.05	224	45.10^2	0.09	104	12.10^2
July 6	0.06	234	39	0.13	180	14
July 27	0.10	316	32	0.22	235	11
August 15	0.18	416	26	0.25	295	12

It is certainly incorrect to assume that one species always contains more of a particular element than does another species or that a herbage sample taken in late summer can indicate what was available in spring or early summer for a grazing animal.

When different plant parts are compared, the position becomes even more complicated, as shown by the results for the zinc content of flowering cocksfoot (Table 8) based on Davey and Mitchell (1968). The uppermost young rachis-node leaves contain eight times as much zinc as the leaves from the lower nodes, while almost half of the zinc in the plant is in the flowerhead. This raises the question of the availability to the animal of trace elements in various parts of the plant. Effects of this type vary from element to element, some displaying little or no differentiation, and from species to species.

The existence of these factors affecting the composition of the vegetation growing on any soil makes it difficult to establish, without

TABLE 8. ZINC CONTENT AND DISTRIBUTION IN DRY MATTER IN FLOWERING COCKSFOOT (DAVEY AND MITCHELL, 1968)

		Zn content (ppm)	Zn contribution (percent)
Whole plant		24	...
Spikelet		50	47.1
Leaf	Rachis	88	10.3
	3rd	34	5.1
	1st + 2nd	11	1.7
Sheath	Rachis	22	5.9
	3rd	11	3.5
	1st + 2nd	10	2.1
Stem	Rachis	15	9.2
	3rd	9	9.1
	1st + 2nd	6	6.0

detailed experimentation, just how much of any element is contained in the food of a grazing animal, even when it is captive and restricted to one soil type. When an animal has free access to several types of soil, or like man, draws only a small fraction of its diet from the soil of the immediate neighborhood, the position is even more difficult. The complexity of the soil distribution that can arise within a relatively small area is illustrated by a soil map from the Aberdeen district of about 400 sq mi around Inverurie (Glentworth and Muir, 1963) where more than 40 different types are mapped on parent materials varying from ultrabasic to acidic igneous rocks and from argillaceous schists or slates to sandstones. Such variability is not exceptional in Scotland.

Despite this, requests are frequently received from medical sources to provide trace-element information applicable to a geographical region covering thousands of square miles, so that the incidence of some disease can be correlated with these generalized soil figures. It should be apparent from the foregoing that this is impracticable, if not impossible, and would appear to be the wrong approach. A more profitable approach would be to correlate information on specific occurrences of such a disease, including precise geographical coordinates, with detailed information concerning the levels of the different trace elements in the soil types at the locations in question. It is planned to store such information on Scottish soils as it becomes available, but a considerable data storage facility, beyond that of the present Institute computer, is required.

REFERENCES CITED

Barber, S. A., Halstead, E. H., and Follett, R. F., 1967, Significant mechanisms controlling the movement of manganese and molybdenum to plant roots growing in soil, *in* Soil chemistry and fertility: Internat. Soc. Soil Sci. Comm. II & IV Trans. (Aberdeen), p. 299–304.

Berrow, M. L., 1958, Studies on the distribution and location of trace elements in soil profiles, [Ph.D. Thesis]: Aberdeen, Scotland, Univ. Aberdeen.

Berrow, M. L., and Webber, J., 1972, Trace elements in sewage sludges: Sci. Food Agric. Jour., v. 23, (in press).

Davey, B. G., and Mitchell, R. L., 1968, The distribution of trace elements in cocksfoot (Dactylis glomerata) at flowering: Sci. Food Agric. Jour., v. 19, p. 425–431.

DeKock, P. C., and Mitchell, R. L., 1957, Uptake of chelated metals by plants: Soil Sci., v. 84, p. 55–62.

Glentworth, R., and Muir, J. W., 1963, The soils of the country round Aberdeen, Inverurie and Fraserburgh: Soil Surv. Mem. Great Britain: Edinburgh, Her Majesty's Stationery Office.

Graham-Bryce, I. J., 1967, The movements of potassium and magnesium ions in soil in relation to their availability, *in* Soil potassium and magnesium: Min. Agric., Fish., and Food Tech. Bull. 14, (London).

Hodgson, J. F., Lindsay, W. L., and Kemper, W. D., 1967, Contributions of fixed charge and mobile complexing agents to the diffusion of Zn: Soil Sci. Soc. America Proc., v. 31, p. 410–413.

Hodgson, J. F., Lindsay, W. L., and Trierwiler, J. F., 1966, Micronutrient cation complexing in soil solution II: Soil Sci. Soc. America Proc., v. 30, p. 723–726.

Mitchell, R. L., 1951, The trace constituents of the soil: 1947 Cong. Pure Appl. Chem. Trans., v. 3, p. 157–164.

—— 1964, Trace elements in soils, *in* Bear, F. E., ed., Chemistry of the soil, 2nd ed.: New York, Reinhold, p. 320–368.

Mitchell, R. L., Reith, J. W. S., and Johnston, I. M., 1957a, Trace-element uptake in relation to soil content: Sci. Food Agric. Jour., v. 8, p. 551–559.

—— 1957b, Soil copper status and plant uptake: Plant analysis and fertilizer problems 2nd Colloq. (Paris) 1956, p. 249–259: Paris, Institut de Recherches pour les Huiles et Oleagineux.

Nye, P. H., 1967, Changes in the concentration of nutrients in the soil near planar absorbing surfaces when simultaneous diffusion and mass flow occur, *in* Soil chemistry and fertility: Internat. Soc. Soil Sci. Commissions II & IV Trans. (Aberdeen), p. 317–327.

Oliver, S., and Barber, S. A., 1966, An evaluation of the mechanisms governing the supply of Ca, Mg, K, and Na to soybean roots: Soil Sci. Soc. America Proc., v. 30, p. 82–86.

Purves, D., 1968, Trace-element contamination of soils in urban areas: 9th Internat. Cong. Soil Sci. Trans. (Adelaide), v. 2, p. 351–355.

Reith, J.W.S., and Mitchell, R. L., 1964, The effect of soil treatment on trace element uptake by plants, *in* Plant analysis and fertilizer problems, 4th Colloq., (Brussels), p. 241–254: New York, American Soc. Horticult. Sci.

Taylor, R. M., and McKenzie, R. M., 1966, The association of trace elements with manganese minerals in Australian soils: Australian Jour. Soil Research, v. 4, p. 29–39.

Williams, E. G., 1962, Chemical soil tests as an aid to increased productivity: Internat. Soc. Soil Sci. Commissions IV & V, Trans. (New Zealand), p. 820–834.

Manuscript Received by the Society June 9, 1971

Published in The Geological Society of America Bulletin, April, 1972.

PRINTED IN U.S.A.

The Geological Society of America, Inc.
Special Paper 140, 1972

Chemical Factors That Influence the Availability of Iron and Manganese in Aqueous Systems

John D. Hem
U.S. Geological Survey, Menlo Park, California 94025

ABSTRACT

The principal factors affecting aqueous chemical behavior of iron and manganese are shown in Eh-pH diagrams, designed to show predominant solute species, stable solid forms and solubility. Simple systems which contain water and the metal, and more complicated systems which contain fixed total amounts of one to four additional anions are considered. Relatively small shifts in Eh or pH can greatly change the equilibrium solubility of the metals. Some complexes, especially ferric fluoride and probably organic ferrous and ferric complexes, may strongly influence the solubility of iron. Because iron and manganese have low solubilities in oxidizing systems at pH levels near or little above neutrality, small shifts in Eh or pH, and complexing effects, may be very important in making the metals available to plants and animals.

OCCURRENCE OF IRON AND MANGANESE IN NATURAL SYSTEMS

Iron and manganese are among the most abundant metals in the surface rock and soil of the earth, but they are generally present in natural water in low concentrations. In this context, low concentrations are considered to be those ranging downward from 1.0 mg/l (milligram per liter). This very broad generalization is valid for many other elements that are essential to living organisms. Capturing the necessary supply of such elements requires chemical alterations or manipulations that will increase the solubility of the element in water, perhaps followed by other chemical changes that will permit the element to be retained. The purpose of this brief discussion is to outline chemical factors that control the solubility of iron and manganese, and to show how the factors are interrelated in ways that are particularly significant in making the elements available to living organisms.

The two elements have some similarity in chemical behavior. Although the analogy should not be overemphasized, most of this paper is concerned with the chemistry of iron: the applicability of similar principles to manganese is demonstrated to show both similarities and differences in behavior.

General behavior traits of iron that are of major significance in considering its solubility and availability include: (1) Iron may occur in the ferric (oxidized) or ferrous (reduced) state, and oxidation or reduction is readily accomplished. (2) Oxidized forms tend to have low solubility, especially in alkaline solutions. (3) Reduced metals can form compounds with carbonate or sulfide that are low in solubility. (4) Organic and inorganic solute complexes are formed with many ligands and this tends to increase the solubilities of iron species. (5) Colloidal dispersions of ferric hydroxide can occur. (6) Iron is essential to living matter and is, therefore, present in biological material that may become available to water as a result of life processes.

Eh-pH DIAGRAMS

A convenient means for evaluating the major features of iron chemistry that influence the solubility is through electrochemical equilibrium calculations, and mass-law solubility calculations. A graphical representation of the relationships developed in these calculations, the Eh-pH diagram, will be used.

Techniques for preparing Eh-pH diagrams have been described in detail in numerous publications (Garrels and Christ, 1965; Hem and Cropper, 1959) and will not be repeated here. The Nernst equation, relating standard oxidation potentials for chemical half-reactions to equilibrium redox potentials (Eh) in the presence of known or assumed activities of participating ions, is the basis for many of the relations in these diagrams. The equation may be written:

$$Eh = E^\circ + \frac{RT}{nF} \ln \frac{[\text{oxidized}]}{[\text{reduced}]},$$

where Eh = redox potential, in volts;

E° = standard potential (25°C, 1 atm, unit activities of solute ions);

R = gas constant;

T = temperature, °K;

n = number of electrons transferred in half-reaction;

F = Faraday constant.

$\ln \frac{[\text{oxidized}]}{[\text{reduced}]}$ = natural logarithm of activities of species in half-reaction, in mass-law form.

In the sign convention used here, oxidizing systems have relatively positive potentials, and reducing systems have negative potentials. Most redox half-reactions involve transfers both of electrons (negative charges) and protons (positively charged H^+). Proton activity in a solution is conveniently measurable by determining the pH.

The range of pH considered in Eh-pH diagrams is generally from 0 to 14. The Eh range of significance in aqueous chemistry is the range in which water is stable, at 1 atm. For convenience, the standard temperature of 25°C is specified throughout this paper. Thermodynamic data for species considered generally has been taken from Wagman and others (1969). Ionic-strength effects are not considered directly. The diagrams are prepared in terms of activities, which correspond to exact concentrations only in infinitely dilute solutions.

The water stability limits with respect to oxidation, forming oxygen gas and H^+, range from 1.23 v at pH 0, to 0.40 v at pH 14. Stability limits for reduction of water to form H_2 gas range from 0.00 v at pH 0 to −0.83 v at pH 14. If a very simple system is specified, containing only iron and water, an Eh-pH diagram can be prepared that will show which solute species of iron will be predominant within the water-stability region.

The pH of natural water is generally within the buffering range of carbon dioxide species, from about pH 5 to about pH 9.5 or 10. The redox potential in water exposed to air is generally from 0.50 to 0.35 v. Oxygen depletion or exposure to anaerobic conditions can decrease the Eh to zero or below. Thus, the area of most significance for natural water is in the lower central two-thirds of the water stability region.

Figure 1 is a diagram showing the regions of dominance for the seven solute species of iron that are expected in the iron-water system. The boundaries of the domains are drawn so that activities of the species on either side of the line are equal. This drawing does not imply that the species shown are completely confined to their respective domains. Actually, some of any species could exist anywhere in the diagram. However, activities of each species decrease rapidly away from the boundaries of its domain.

There are three ferric species shown, two of which are hydroxy complexes, and three ferrous species, also including two hydroxy complexes. One of the latter is anionic. The seventh form shown is the ferrate ion, FeO_4^{-2}, where the oxidation state of iron is +6. Neither of the anionic species has much geochemical signifi-

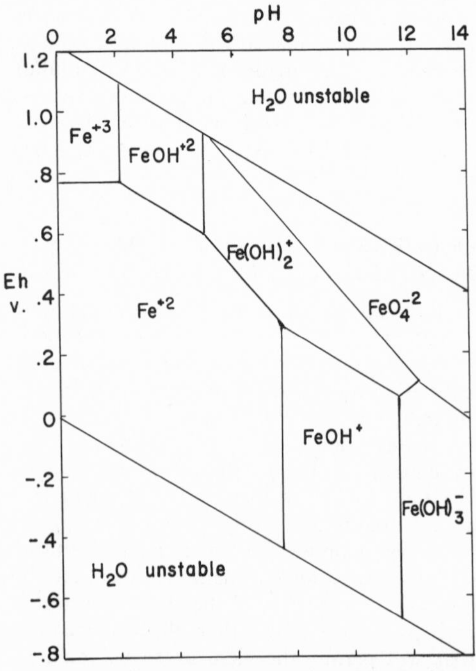

Figure 1. Areas of dominance for solute species as a function of pH and redox potential in the system Fe-H_2O at 25°C and 1 atm.

cance, as both require a higher pH to attain dominance than is usual in natural systems. The ferrate ion particularly is of slight geochemical significance.

Some investigators have reported the existence of the uncharged species $Fe(OH)_3$ aq. and $Fe(OH)_2$ aq. Both would have a fixed solubility throughout their areas of dominance. However, both species have low solubilities (in the vicinity of 0.01 mg/l Fe) and can be omitted from the diagram without serious error unless very low total iron concentrations are being considered. Dimeric or polynuclear ferric hydroxide complex ions are also known, but do not become predominant unless dissolved iron concentrations are very high (>1,000 mg/l). Thus, although no specific solubility limits were involved in calculating the positions of the boundaries in Figure 1, the choice of solute species does limit the applicability of the diagram to a solubility range.

By considering solute and solid species simultaneously a more useful Eh-pH diagram for iron can be constructed. Figure 2 is an Eh-pH diagram for a system similar to that of Figure 1; however, it utilizes single specified concentrations of dissolved iron to locate stability regions

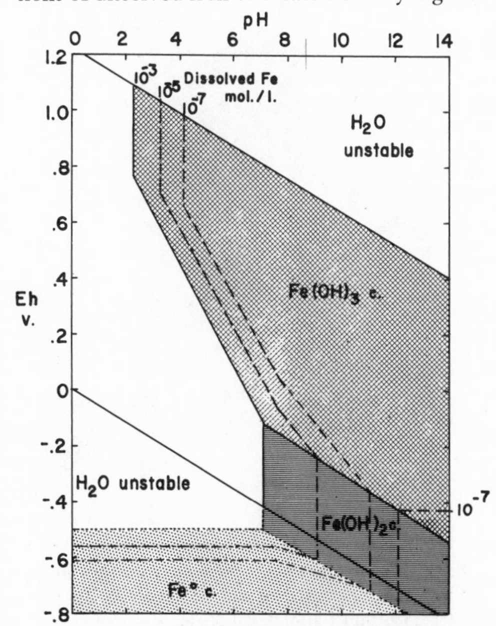

Figure 2. Stability fields for solids as a function of pH and redox potential in the system Fe-H_2O at 25°C and 1 atm. Activity of dissolved iron 10^{-3} mol/l (56 mg/l Fe). Positions of stability-field boundaries for [Fe] = 10^{-5} and 10^{-7} mol/l are indicated by dashed lines.

for solids. The ferric hydroxide stability region (cross-hatched) extends through much of the region where the Eh and pH of natural aerated water would be. Ferrous hydroxide $Fe(OH)_2$ would be the stable solid at high pH in a reducing environment. A stability region for metallic iron occurs below the dashed boundary and outside the water stability region. The location of this field shows why iron is so susceptible to corrosion.

The dehydrated forms of iron oxide including hematite and magnetite are much less soluble than the species shown here, but they are evidently not the controlling forms in most natural aqueous systems.

The shaded regions of Figure 2 represent areas where iron has a relatively low solubility, although the outer limits shown are arbitrary and depend on the activity of iron species that is used in the calculation. The limits shown by shading are for a total iron activity of 10^{-3} mol/l equivalent to 56 mg/l Fe. The dashed lines show how the solid stability regions would shrink at the lower activities of 10^{-5} and 10^{-7} molar (0.56 mg/l and 5.6 μg/l).

Some investigators have reported mixed ferrous-ferric hydroxides. For example, Ponnamperuma and others (1967) state that $Fe_3(OH)_8$ is present in water-saturated soils. Species considered in Figure 2 are the ones for which thermodynamic data are given by Wagman and others (1969), with a few minor exceptions where data used by the writer in earlier publications (Hem and Cropper, 1959) seem to fit observable conditions more closely. The choice of solid species is arbitrary, and it should be recognized that natural iron hydroxides will not be pure and will have a variable degree of crystalline organization. As a result, the conditions in natural systems may differ somewhat from theoretical ones presented here. For iron occurring in ground-water systems, the theoretical values given here have been found by other investigators (Back and Barnes, 1965) to be reasonably satisfactory.

Most natural water contains enough of the common anions to influence the behavior of iron somewhat; hence, a more complete diagram will be more useful in considering the behavior of iron in river or underground water. Contact with air causes solution of carbon dioxide, usually in the form of bicarbonate ions. Natural water also contains sulfur, usually in oxidized form as sulfate ions, but potentially reducible to sulfide species, and also contains chloride and fluoride ions. Some of these ions may combine with iron to produce solids of low solubility. Examples include ferrous carbonate (siderite) and ferrous disulfide (pyrite). The latter is stable in reduced environments. Or the anions may combine with iron to give stable solute complexes that yield additional solute domains like the ones shown in Figure 1.

Figure 3 shows the domains of solute species in an iron-water system to which fluoride anions have been added. There are two strong ferric fluoride complexes in the specified system, FeF_2^+ and FeF^{+2}. Their domains are shown by solid lines for a total fluoride activity of 10^{-3} mol/l (19 mg/l) and by dashed lines for 10^{-4} mol/l (1.9 mg/l). The total activity of iron is presumed to be relatively low (10^{-5} or less). The effect of the higher fluoride concentration is to extend substantially the Eh-pH region where ferric solute species are dominant, and at this concentration the fields for Fe^{+3} and $FeOH^+$ are eliminated. At the lower fluoride content there is a small remnant of the Fe^{+3} field at very low pH where most of the fluoride would be present as undissociated hydrofluoric acid, HF°. Fluoride concentrations in natural water generally are below 1.0 mg/l, but some relatively dilute waters may contain as much as 50 mg/l (Hem, 1970, p. 178).

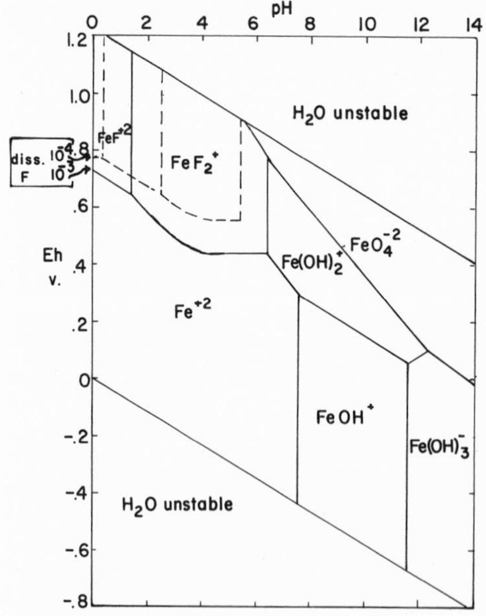

Figure 3. Areas of dominance for solute species as a function of pH and redox potential in system Fe-F-H_2O at 25°C and 1 atm. Total dissolved activity of F 10^{-3} mol/l (19 mg/l) and 10^{-4} mol/l (1.9 mg/l).

Although some other complexes of iron are formed with the ligands present in major amounts in natural water, the complexing action is generally rather weak and less likely to affect the behavior of the metal than are the fluoride complexes. The higher complex with fluoride FeF_3 is not likely to be predominant because this requires more than 10^{-3} mol/l of fluoride. Chloride complexes with ferric iron are very much weaker than fluoride species and are not important up to chloride concentrations near those of sea water. A ferrous sulfate complex and several ferric sulfate complexes are possible if sulfate concentrations are high enough. Generally these species will not be significant unless sulfate concentrations approach or exceed 1,000 mg/l as SO_4^{-2}.

Many natural waters contain considerable concentrations of anions, and it is interesting to observe the effect these higher concentrations might have on the behavior of iron. Figure 4 represents a system containing carbon dioxide

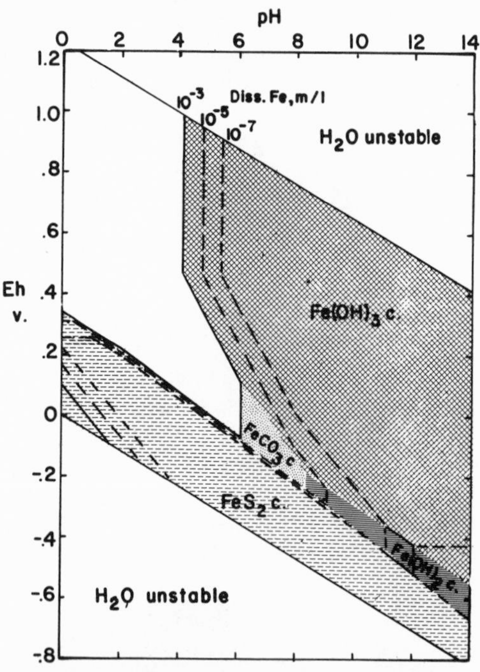

Figure 4. Stability fields for solids as a function of pH and redox potential in the system Fe-F-Cl-S-CO_2-H_2O at 25°C and 1 atm. Total dissolved activities specified 10^{-3} mol/l for F (19 mg/l) and CO_2 (equivalent to 61 mg/l HCO_3^-) and 10^{-2} mol/l for Cl (355 mg/l) and S (equivalent to 960 mg/l SO_4^{-2}). Shaded areas represent stability boundaries for dissolved Fe activity equals 10^{-3} mol/l (56 mg/l). Dashed lines show positions of boundaries at Fe activity of 10^{-5} and 10^{-7} mol/l.

and fluoride species equivalent to 10^{-3} molar, and chloride and sulfur concentrations of 10^{-2} molar. This would give activities of about 61 mg/l HCO_3, 19 mg/l F, 355 mg/l Cl, and 960 mg/l SO_4. These, of course, would need to be balanced by other cations besides iron, but they could be nonparticipating species, such as sodium. This solution would be somewhat above the concentrations usually considered as satisfactory for potable water, yet many natural waters have as great or greater concentrations. At pH 7.00 and 25°C, an activity of 61 mg/l of HCO_3 would be in equilibrium with a partial pressure of carbon dioxide of 6.8×10^{-3} atm. The diagram shows stability regions for solids at activities of iron of 10^{-3} mol/l and as in Figure 2, the positions of lower solubility boundaries for iron are indicated by dashed lines.

Figure 4 indicates a small stability region for siderite ($FeCO_3$) and a large field for pyrite; although a narrow $Fe(OH)_2$ region remains, it has mostly disappeared. The predominant solute species along the $Fe(OH)_3$ and $FeCO_3$ boundaries are the ferric fluoride complex FeF_2^+ and the ferrous sulfate complex $FeSO_4$ aq.

Figure 4 suggests the greatest solubility for iron is in the moderately reducing environment unless the solution has a very low pH. In general, the effect of increased bicarbonate or sulfur activity would be to enlarge the stability regions of siderite or pyrite at the expense of adjacent areas. Increased activity of solute complexes of iron would tend to increase the solubility of iron, other factors remaining equal.

Although iron is shown to be readily available to organisms in mildly reducing environments near neutral pH, the balance between an adequate and an inadequate supply may be delicate, and minor pH changes or oxidation-potential changes may bring about deficiencies.

The Eh-pH diagram can only represent systems that have reached chemical equilibrium. Application of the diagram to natural systems generally requires the assumption of a close approach to equilibrium. Most of the oxidation and reduction reactions of iron in the near-neutral pH range are relatively rapid and reversible, however, and it is not unreasonable to assume equilibrium for the iron species in natural water (Hem, 1960). The reversibility of some of the reactions involving iron appears to be an important factor in the biochemical roles of the element.

Actual measurements of oxidation and reduction rates of iron in aerated water have been made by some investigators. Stumm and Lee (1961) found the rate of oxidation of ferrous ions in aerated water to be increased 100-fold by raising the pH one unit. This oxidation is extremely slow in strongly acid solutions. The rate is affected by bicarbonate and sulfate concentrations and also by dissolved silica (Weber and Schenk, 1968). Oxidation processes are used in treatment of water supplies to remove objectionable concentrations of ferrous iron.

Both ferrous and ferric iron can form strong complex ions with organic ligands. Many natural systems contain organic solutes that could form such complexes with iron. The behavior of iron in soils is probably particularly strongly affected by organic complexes, because the organic solute concentration of soil moisture can be rather large.

Complex ions normally tend to increase the solubility of the metal, because the total solubility is a summation of all the various solute species that can exist at equilibrium. Although most organic ligands can be destroyed by strong oxidation, some species of organic-iron complexes do, no doubt, have a sufficient stability to influence equilibrium solubility. An indirect influence can also be present because complexed iron may react more slowly than uncomplexed species, and thus change the behavior of the metal substantially.

Eh-pH diagrams are useful for other metals whose chemical behavior is affected by oxidation and reduction. Manganese is considered as an example, using an approach similar to that used for iron, and based on earlier work by the writer (Hem, 1963).

The manganese-water system is shown in Figure 5 at standard conditions of temperature and pressure. The diagram shows regions of stability for solids and the solubility of manganese as well as the dominant solute forms. Manganese has three oxidation states that need consideration in the water stability region, the +2, +3, and +4 forms. Oxides shown in Figure 5 include MnO_2 (pyrolusite), Mn_2O_3 and Mn_3O_4, and the manganous hydroxide $Mn(OH)_2$ is also a stable form at low Eh. Solute complexes considered include $MnOH^+$ and $HMnO_2^-$.

In comparison with the corresponding diagram for the iron-water system, it is evident that manganese is considerably more soluble than iron in the Eh-pH range of principal interest. The large area in which Mn^{+2} is the domi-

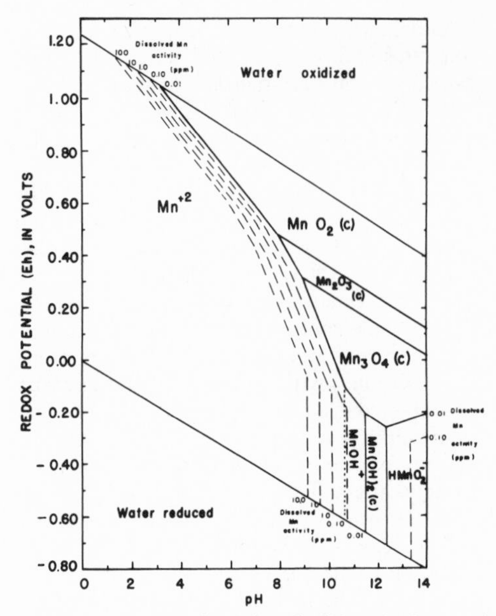

Figure 5. Fields of stability of solids and solutes and solubility of manganese as functions of pH and redox potential at 25°C and 1 atm in system Mn-H_2O.

nant solute form is also of interest. Naturally occurring manganese oxides commonly are mixtures of species with numerous impurities, and the theoretical solubilities for manganese do not always agree closely with observed values. In general, however, the calculations furnish almost as good an approximation of solubility in natural conditions as do the diagrams for iron.

Introduction of other anions into the manganese-water system adds new solids and solute complexes. Figure 6 is for a system containing bicarbonate species activity equivalent to 2,000 mg/l HCO_3^- ($10^{-1.48}$ mol/l). Besides introducing a large field of stability for $MnCO_3$ there is also a solute complex, $MnHCO_3^+$, whose effect is important. The stability boundary of MnO_2 is bulged somewhat by the complexing effect. There is also a sulfate complex. Its influence is indicated in Figure 7 where the system considered has the equivalent of 2,000 mg/l activity of SO_4 ($10^{-1.68}$ mol/l). The influence of solute complexes on behavior of manganese seems to be less important than for iron, and rather high concentrations of ligands are required to show the effects on an Eh-pH diagram. Manganese complexes with chloride and fluoride are of negligible significance.

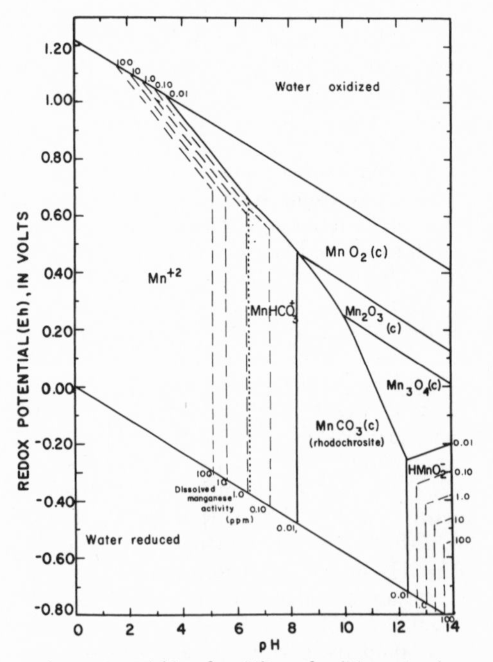

Figure 6. Fields of stability of solids and solutes and solubility of manganese as functions of pH and redox potential at 25°C and 1 atm in system Mn-CO_2-H_2O. Bicarbonate species activity 2,000 mg/l as HCO_3.

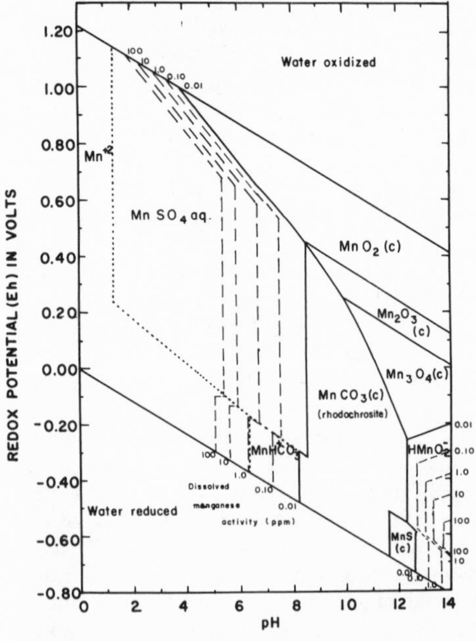

Figure 7. Fields of stability of solids and solutes and solubility of manganese as functions of pH and redox potential at 25°C and 1 atm in system Mn-S-CO_2-H_2O. Total CO_2 species activity 2,000 mg/l as HCO_3^-, total sulfur species activity 2,000 mg/l as SO_4^{-2}.

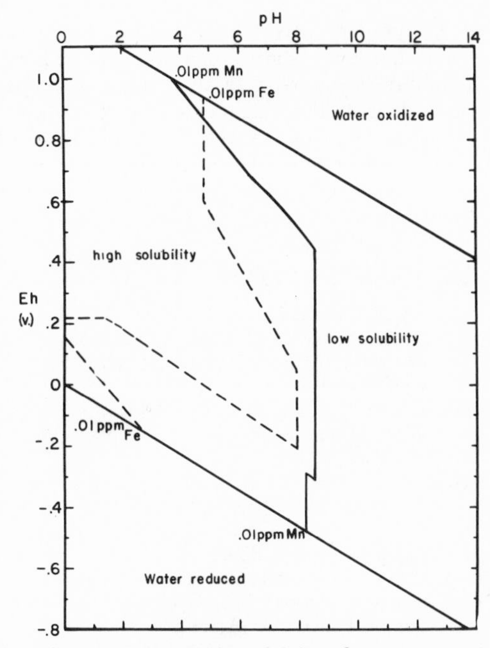

Figure 8. Comparative solubility of manganese and iron in system H_2O-Mn-Fe-CO_2-S-H_2O at 25°C and 1 atm. Total CO_2 species activity 2,000 mg/l as HCO_3^-, total sulfur species activity 2,000 mg/l as SO_4^{-2}.

A general comparison of manganese and iron solubilities is given in Figure 8, where the bicarbonate and sulfate activities are the same as in Figure 7. The dashed line, showing solubility of iron indicates that for almost any Eh and pH within the water stability field, more manganese will be in solution than iron will be at equilibrium. Interactions among manganese and iron species may occur where both metals are present in the same system. Figure 8 is not intended to represent that kind of system.

CHEMICAL CONTROLS OF SOLUBILITY

From the Eh-pH diagrams and related calculations, it is possible to generalize about the relative importance of different chemical controls of metal solubilities and to speculate briefly about the manner in which metals might most readily become available, through increased solubility, for uptake by plants or utilization by animals. It is convenient to utilize the relations developed for iron for these generalizations.

Iron can be made more or less soluble in a particular system through at least six different mechanisms:

1. Solubility of iron may be changed by changing pH. At the boundary between ferric hydroxide and dissolved ferrous iron, the equilibrium equation is

$$Eh = 1.057 - 0.0592 \log [Fe^{+2}] - 0.178\, pH\,.$$

For a given Eh value a change of one tenth pH unit in the vicinity of pH 7 will change the equilibrium solubility of iron by about a factor of 2. Obviously this can be a delicately balanced system. Many natural waters are subject to changes caused by photosynthesis and other factors that can cause variations in pH approaching or exceeding a full unit during a 24-hr period. Thus adjustment of pH would appear to be a very effective means for controlling iron solubility.

2. Solubility of iron may be changed by changing Eh. The mechanisms available for altering redox potential can greatly alter iron solubility. For example, if the oxygen were depleted by a factor of 10 in originally oxygenated water, and if the oxygen-water system controls the potential, the effect would be to lower the Eh by about 0.03 v, which represents a change in iron solubility (increase) by a factor of about 3.

3. If other factors are held constant, increased or decreased activity of certain anions will change iron solubility. For example, if the bicarbonate activity is decreased in the siderite stability region, the solubility of ferrous iron will increase by a directly equivalent amount. A change in this anion probably would also affect the pH.

4. Solubility of iron may be increased by increasing the activity of a complexing ligand. The ferric fluoride complex used in preparing Figure 4 increases the solubility of iron many orders of magnitude near pH 6 in the oxidizing region. The effect of increasing total fluoride activity from 10^{-4} to 10^{-3} molar is to increase iron solubility a hundredfold, provided that the fluoride ion remains in excess.

A particularly intriguing aspect of complexing effects relates to the possible influence of ferrous complexes on solubility of iron in the vicinity of neutral pH. Thermodynamic data are available for some of the species of interest. The ferrous hydroxide and ferrous sulfate complexes were considered in drawing the Eh-pH diagrams for this paper. There are few strong inorganic ferrous complexes, and generally ferric complexes with both organic and inorganic ligands are stronger than the corresponding ferrous ones. Some of the organic complexing ligands, however, are capable of forming strong ferrous complexes.

Natural waters probably can contain concentrations of organic complex-forming substances up to about 10^{-4} mol/l (Semenov and others, 1967), although very few actual analytical data on such specific organic substances in natural water are available. Assuming 1 to 1 complexing, where the first step stability constant for the complex with ferrous iron is about 10^4, the effect might be sufficient to double the solubility of iron compared to the uncomplexed value, where solubility is controlled by a redox reaction involving ferric hydroxide. Stability constants for organic ferrous complexes given by Sillén and Martell (1964) range up as high as 10^{18}, but most of the stronger complexes probably involve organic molecules that are unlikely to be abundant in natural water. Soil moisture, plant sap, and fluids in animal tissues, or river water that contains large amounts of organic waste, may of course have very large amounts of organic materials with possible complexing effects.

There is a tendency for both iron and manganese to occur in water as finely divided particles of hydroxide. Adsorbed organic solutes are believed by some to exert a physical stabilizing effect on such colloidal suspensions. This type of combination of organics with metals is not the same as the complexing that produces actual ions in solution. Particulate suspended material is not readily available for use by organisms, in any event, and this kind of effect is not worth further consideration here.

5. Solubility can be altered from values given here by changes in temperature or pressure to values other than 25°C and 1 atm. The data are not adequate for complete evaluation of temperature effects; the effects within normal earth conditions near the surface are probably substantially smaller than those indicated for the first four mechanisms.

6. Departure from equilibrium can be produced by energy input from other sources. Although this is man's favorite approach to obtain what he wants from nature, it is not always usable by other life forms. Solar energy can be captured by photosynthesis and may be stored and used in other ways by plants and animals.

In general, although the above evaluation shows the formation of soluble complexes to be a very effective means of increasing iron solubility, the complexed iron may become stabilized to the point that it is not readily useful for a need required by an organism.

In summary, it is evident that iron (and to a somewhat lesser degree, manganese) has a low-equilibrium solubility in aerated water in the neutral or mildly alkaline pH range. Soluble forms of the metals are the only kinds that can be utilized directly in plant or animal metabolism. Thus, the chemical nature of the environment may be a critical factor in availability of these essential metals.

REFERENCES CITED

Back, William, and Barnes, Ivan, 1965, Relation of electrochemical potentials and iron content to ground water flow patterns: U.S. Geol. Survey Prof. Paper 498–C, p. C13.

Garrels, R. M., and Christ, C. L., 1965, Solutions, minerals and equilibria: New York, Harper and Row, p. 172–266.

Hem, J. D., 1960, Restraints on dissolved ferrous iron imposed by bicarbonate, redox potential, and *p*H: U.S. Geol. Survey Water-Supply Paper 1459–B, p. 33–55.

—— 1963, Chemical equilibria and rates of manganese oxidation: U.S. Geol. Survey Water-Supply Paper 1667–A, 64 p.

—— 1970, Study and interpretation of chemical characteristics of natural water (2d ed.): U.S. Geol. Survey Water-Supply Paper 1473, 363 p.

Hem, J. D., and Cropper, W. H., 1959, Survey of ferrous-ferric chemical equilibria and redox potentials: U.S. Geol. Survey Water-Supply Paper 1459–A, 31 p.

Ponnamperuma, F. N., Tianco, E. M., and Loy, Teresita, 1967, Redox equilibria in flooded soils: 1. The iron hydroxide system: Soil Sci., v. 103, p. 374.

Semenov, A. D., Pashanova, A. P., Kishkinova, T. S., and Nemetseva, L. I., 1967, Content of individual groups of organic substances in the waters of some Soviet rivers [trans.]: Soviet Hydrology, Selected Papers no. 5, p. 549–554.

Sillén, L. G., and Martell, A. E., 1964, Stability constants of metal-ion complexes: Chem. Soc. [London] Spec. Pub. 17, 754 p.

Stumm, Werner, and Lee, G. F., 1961, Oxygenation of ferrous iron: Indus. and Eng. Chemistry, v. 53, p. 143–146.

Wagman, D. C., Evans, W. H., Parker, V. B., Halow, I., Baily, S. M., and Schumm, R. H., 1969, Selected values of chemical thermodynamic properties: Natl. Bur. Standards Tech. Note 270–4, 141 p.

Weber, W. J., Jr., and Schenk, J. E., 1968, Chemical interaction of dissolved silica with iron (II) and (III): Am. Water Works Assoc. Jour., v. 60, p. 199–212.

Manuscript Received by the Society June 9, 1971

Publication Authorized by the Director, U.S. Geological Survey

Published in The Geological Society of America Bulletin, February, 1972.

PRINTED IN U.S.A.

The Geological Society of America, Inc.
Special Paper 140, 1972

Iron and Associated Trace Mineral Problems in Man and Animals

James C. Fritz
*Division of Nutrition, Food and Drug Administration,
Department of Health, Education, and Welfare, Washington, D. C. 20204*

ABSTRACT

There is a high incidence of iron-deficiency anemia in the United States and throughout the world. The prevalence is high in adult women and infants because of their greater needs for iron. The typical human diet furnishes less than 6 mg iron per 1,000 kcal and does not meet the current recommended dietary allowances for critical groups because so much of the iron in whole, raw foodstuffs is removed in processing. Farm animals fare better because they receive fractions removed from human foods. A few livestock groups, notably baby pigs, do need supplemental iron.

The cereal enrichment program failed to alleviate human anemia because of reduced consumption of cereals and because poorly utilized sources of supplemental iron were employed. Ferric orthophosphate and sodium iron pyrophosphate were poorly utilized by chicks, rats, and humans. Ferrous sulfate was well utilized by each of the three species, while reduced iron was intermediate. The source of supplemental iron had more influence on bioavailability than did other diet components. It is recommended that the level of iron be increased in enriched cereals, that milk and other foods be fortified with iron, and that iron sources with good bioavailability be used in the fortification program.

INTRODUCTION

In spite of the fact that iron is one of the more abundant elements on earth, we have a high prevalence of iron deficiency anemia in the United States (Am. Med. Assoc., 1968) and throughout the world (WHO, 1968). This is due chiefly to insufficient intake of iron to meet the dietary needs of women and children (Agric. Res. Service, 1969). Changing food habits and changing methods of food preparation have reduced the consumption of food iron (Peden, 1967).

The cereal enrichment program has not helped the situation, and the prevalence of iron deficiency anemia is fully as high as it was 30 yrs ago (Gutelius, 1969). The reasons for failure of the cereal enrichment program in this respect include (a) reduced consumption of cereals, (b) enrichment levels that were too low, and (c) use of poorly utilized sources of supplemental iron.

Measures to improve the situation regarding iron in nutrition are available. Additional foods should be fortified with iron. A special effort should be made to add iron to those foods that are consumed in quantity by the population. This includes fortification of milk because this would increase the iron intake of young children (Gutelius, 1969). A petition to increase the enrichment level in cereals has been published (Fed. Regist., 1970). Only sources of iron with acceptable biological availability should be used for food fortification (Pla and Fritz, 1970).

NUTRITIONAL ANEMIA

Many surveys have shown that anemia is one of the most prevalent of the nutritional deficiency diseases (Am. Med. Assoc., 1968; WHO, 1968; Gutelius, 1969; Goldsmith, 1965; Schaefer, 1969; White, 1970). While there are many possible causes of anemia, it is believed that the most common cause is iron deficiency. Some of the factors that aggravate the condition are those that drain more iron from the body through loss of blood. These include menstrual losses in women, parasitic infection, and hemorrhage from any cause. Of the estimated 4 to 5 g of iron in the adult body, about three-quarters is in the red blood cells, chiefly bound to protein as hemoglobin and myoglobin (Underwood, 1962).

The usual criteria for diagnosis of anemia are hemoglobin and hematocrit levels. If the anemia is hypochromic and microcytic, it is probably due to iron deficiency. Measurements of plasma iron, iron-binding capacity, and percent saturation of transferrin can be used to further identify the cause of the anemia (Fomon, 1970). Hemoglobin values below 10 g per 100 ml of blood and hematocrit values below 31 percent packed cell volume can be considered indicative of severe anemia. Many authorities use higher cut-off values (Am. Med. Assoc., 1968; WHO, 1968).

An important point to remember is that the body has other uses for iron in addition to hemoglobin formation. It has been demonstrated that other body stores of iron are depleted before the hemoglobin level falls. Concern has been expressed about iron-deficiency in tissues such as liver, spleen, and bone marrow before anemia occurs (White, 1970; Beal, 1970). Measurements of hemoglobin and hematocrit detect only advanced cases of iron deficiency.

There is no general agreement about the effect of anemia on health. There is evidence that anemic children have less resistance to infection and that they are more prone to complications (Gutelius, 1969a). In baby pigs, untreated iron-deficiency anemia results in heavy death losses (Natl. Acad. Sci., 1968a).

The prevalence of anemia is highest among pregnant women and young children. The American Medical Association Committee on Iron Deficiency (1968) summarized data which showed from 15 to 58 percent of the pregnant women had hemoglobin values considered to indicate anemia. The World Health Organization report (1968a) found the following proportion of the cases studied to be anemic:

Country	Percent of pregnant women who were anemic
Israel	47.0
Poland	21.8
India (Delhi)	80.0
India (Vellore)	56.0
Mexico	26.6
Venezuela	37.0

Fomon (1970) has pointed out that the incidence of anemia in infants varies widely in different areas. The different studies reported showed a range extending from virtually none to as many as 76 percent of the infants with hemoglobin levels below 10 grams per 100 ml. Poverty areas and groups have a higher incidence of anemia. Zee and others (1970) found 28 percent of the children up to 3 yrs of age from impoverished Memphis families to have hemoglobin levels below 10 g per 100 ml. Gutelius (1969) found that the incidence of anemia among the children in a Washington, D.C., clinic increased to 1.5 yrs of age and then decreased as the children became older. The group between 12 and 17 months of age had an average hemoglobin value of only 9.11 g per 100 ml, and more than 65 percent of these infants had hemoglobin values below 10 g per 100 ml.

REQUIREMENT FOR IRON

The most recent edition of Recommended Dietary Allowances (Natl. Acad. Sci., 1968b) shows increased levels of iron for several groups that are prone to nutritional anemia. The recommended daily intake for women was raised to 18 mg. This is based on estimates of iron losses from the body, and on the assumption that 10 percent of the iron consumed will be absorbed. The many variables make any suggested allowance only a crude approximation. Hegsted (1970) has reviewed some of the problems involved, and notes that not all women will have their iron requirements met by an intake of 18 mg per day or by any reasonable dietary level.

Estimates of the dietary iron requirements (Am. Med. Assoc., 1968) are about as follows:

Group	Absorbed iron required per day (mg)	Daily food iron required (mg)
Men and non-menstruating women	0.5–1.0	5–10
Menstruating women	0.7–2.0	7–20
Pregnant women	2.0–4.8	20–48
Adolescents	1.0–2.0	10–20
Children	0.4–1.0	4–10
Infants	0.5–1.5	5–15

The basic body needs for iron are not large as will be discussed further by Dr. Hopps. The greater need is for growth, replacement of blood losses, and fetal development. The problem is compounded when we try to meet the needs through foods that will be consumed in varying quantities by all groups regardless of their iron requirements.

The iron requirements for domestic animals are ordinarily met by the usual feedstuffs.

However, there is a problem in meeting the needs of baby pigs (Natl. Acad. Sci., 1968a); a minimum of 80 mg iron per kg of the pig's diet is recommended. Most other domestic animals have their requirements met with much less iron. The problem of furnishing laying hens with enough iron to meet their needs may require some attention as each egg contains about 1.1 mg iron. The use of high energy laying rations makes it essential that such diets contain at least 80 mg iron per kg to meet the needs of hens in heavy production.

FOOD IRON

The cereal grains generally are fairly good sources of iron. The following estimates for the iron content of several whole grains are taken chiefly from U.S. Department of Agriculture Handbook No. 8 (Watt and others, 1963):

Cereal grain	Iron content (mg/kg)
Barley	27
Buckwheat	31
Corn	24
Oats	35
Rice	16
Rye	37
Wheat	35

Special note should be made of a cereal type seed, named teff, grown in Ethiopia where it serves as the chief cereal in the native diet. It is unusually high in vitamins and iron. Representative analyses indicate that teff contains 1,050 mg iron per kg. Even though later studies showed that half to three-quarters of this iron may be due to soil contamination, teff is inherently high in iron (Hofvander, 1968). Ordinarily cereals grown on high iron soils do not contain unusual quantities of iron.

Meats are fairly good sources of iron, generally ranging from about 12 to 33 mg per kg. Organs are usually higher in iron, and livers of various species are reported to contain from 65 to 192 mg per kg (Watt and others, 1963). Legumes are good sources of iron, but most fruits and vegetables are low in iron, and boiling them in liberal amounts of water may further reduce the iron content (Underwood, 1962).

Milk deserves special consideration because it constitutes such a large part of the diet of the young. The iron concentration in the milk of human beings, cows and goats is only about 0.5 mg per l. A few other species do produce milk with higher iron content (Thomas, 1970), but their milk is used only for their own nursing young. The colostrum is somewhat higher in iron than is regular milk. Increasing the iron content of the diet does not increase the iron content of the milk produced by humans, cattle, or swine (Thomas, 1970).

Human infants raised chiefly on milk develop a high incidence of anemia. Gutelius (1969b) explains the high incidence of infant anemia in her studies: "Infants in underprivileged families tend to get too much milk because it is the easiest and quickest food to give them, but milk contains very little iron. . . . Although infants tend to recover after several years from iron deficiency anemia, it is not a condition to be ignored."

Baby pigs, unless given oral or parenteral iron to supplement the sow's milk, become severely anemic, develop the condition known as thumps, and, in many cases, die. It should be noted that this anemia develops in the nursing pigs in spite of the fact that the sow's milk contains 2 to 3 mg of iron per l (Natl. Acad. Sci., 1968a; Thomas, 1970)—several times as much iron as is present in the milk of either human or cow.

We have considered the quantity of iron present in the raw, whole food. What happens when the food is processed and cooked? On the one hand, we may remove much of the inherent iron by refining the food to suit human tastes. On the other hand we may add iron from processing and cooking equipment.

Different types of wheat contain from about 30 to about 43 mg iron per kg. This is concentrated in the outer layers and in the germ. Bran contains about 149 mg iron per kg, shorts or middlings about 95 mg per kg, and the germ about 94 mg per kg. Whole wheat flour contains 33 mg iron per kg, 80 percent extraction flour contains 13 mg; white patent flour has only 8 mg (Watt and others, 1963). The cereal enrichment program, to date, has aimed at restoring to the refined cereal products the whole grain levels of iron and certain B vitamins (Code Federal Regul., 1970). Practices in Great Britain (British Minist. Health, 1968) and in the Scandinavian countries (Höglund and Reizenstein, 1968) generally followed those of the United States.

Iron from processing equipment and from cooking utensils may add substantial quantities to the food. Let us compare the reported average iron content of dried milk products sold for human food with similar products sold for animal feed use:

Dried milk product	mg iron per kg of product	
	NRC feed data*	USDA human food data†
Dried whole milk	174	5
Dried skim milk	52	6
Dried whey	157	14

* Natl. Acad. Sci., 1969
† Watt and others, 1963

Obviously, the high levels of iron in feed grades of dried milk products do not originate in the milk itself. They are "supplemented" in large measure by tramp iron from the processing equipment. Ammerman and others (1970) recently showed that grinding citrus pulp in a Wiley mill raised the iron content by more than 43 percent. Human foods contain less iron than formerly because utensils and machines formerly made of iron are now made of aluminum, stainless steel, and plastics.

The net result of the many changes in our food habits has been a reduction in the iron content of our diet. The problem and its many ramifications are best understood if we look at the iron content of the typical diet in terms of the energy content. Miller (1969, written commun.) has calculated that if the normal diet contains unenriched cereals it will have about 4.6 mg iron per 1,000 kcal. If all standardized cereals are enriched to present standards of identity (Code Federal Regul., 1970), the diet will have about 5.9 mg iron per 1,000 kcal. Natvig (1969) estimates that most European diets supply between 5 and 6 mg iron per 1,000 kcal, but that the Norwegian diet supplies less than 5 mg per 1,000 kcal.

The difficulty of trying to meet fully the iron needs through cereal enrichment is illustrated by the following table, which relates the actual iron intake at different levels of cereal enrichment with the recommended dietary allowances for iron (Natl. Acad. Sci., 1968b) (Table 1).

People eat to satisfy their energy requirements, and the iron needs are not closely related to caloric needs. While the proposal to approximately triple the iron level in standardized cereals (Federal Regist., 1970) would obviously help, such changes would not in themselves assure enough iron for young children and for adult women. Other sources of dietary iron must be sought.

BIOLOGICAL AVAILABILITY OF IRON

It should be obvious that the mere presence of an element in the food does not assure that it is biologically available to the animal that eats that food. We recently studied the bioavailability of a number of iron sources that are, or might be, used for food fortification (Fritz and others, 1970). Hemoglobin repletion in anemic chicks and rats was used as the criterion of availability (Pla and Fritz, 1970), and the results were expressed in terms of the relative biological value with iron from ferrous sulfate used as the reference standard.

Relative biological value =

$$100 \times \frac{\text{mg Fe/kg from FeSO}_4}{\text{mg Fe/kg from sample}}$$

for equal curative effect.

All comparisons were made at suboptimal levels, and the anemic test animals used from 45 to 51 percent of the iron supplied by ferrous sulfate for the formation of new hemoglobin.

Iron sources that showed a relative biological value greater than 70 were considered good sources, and these included the following: dihydrogen ferrous salt of EDTA, ferric ammonium citrate, ferric choline citrate, ferric citrate, ferric fructose, ferric glycerophosphate, ferrilactin, ferric sulfate, ferrous ammonium sulfate, ferrous chloride, ferrous citrate, fer-

Table 1. Iron Requirements Through Cereal Enrichment

Group	Recommended dietary allowance		Iron intake (mg/day)		
	Energy (kcal)	Iron (mg)	4.6 mg per Mcal	5.9 mg per Mcal	8.5 mg per Mcal
Child, 1–2 yrs	1100	15	5.06	6.49	9.35
Child, 2–3 yrs	1250	15	5.75	7.37	10.62
Child, 3–4 yrs	1400	10	6.44	8.26	11.90
Men, 22–35 yrs	2800	10	12.88	16.52	23.80
Women, 22–35 yrs	2000	18	9.20	11.80	17.00

rous fumarate, ferrous gluconate, ferrous sulfate, ferrous tartrate, isolated soybean protein, and black-strap molasses.

Iron sources that showed a relative biological value between 20 and 70 were considered mediocre sources, and these included the following: alfalfa meal, blood meal, cereals enriched with reduced iron, corn germ meal, eggs, ferric chloride, ferric pyrophosphate, fish protein concentrate, reduced iron, oat flour, and wheat germ meal.

Iron sources with a relative biological value less than 20 were considered poor sources, and these included the following: ferric orthophosphate, ferric oxide, ferrous carbonate ores, smectite-vermiculite, and sodium iron pyrophosphate.

Among the poorly utilized iron compounds are two widely used food fortifications: ferric orthophosphate and sodium iron pyrophosphate. Ferrous carbonate ores are widely used for feed fortification, but our tests show them to be of little or no value. Most samples of reduced iron (also called ferrum reductum or ferrum redactum) showed mediocre availability. Different samples of reduced iron vary in their biological availability (Hinton and Moran, 1967) due, at least in part, to the particle size (Höglund and Reizenstein, 1968; Widhe, 1970). Particle size of 10 microns or less is desirable for best biological availability, but such samples tend to discolor the cereals to which they are added. More research is needed to define optimum particle size and other characteristics of reduced iron.

Use of ferrous sulfate is recommended for all food fortification applications where its use is technically feasible. The usual form is the dried, or exsiccated, ferrous sulfate. Of the iron sources commonly used for cereal enrichment, ferrous sulfate is the only one that shows a high relative biological value. It has the disadvantage of being hygroscopic and is reported to cause rancidity in flour and other cereals that are subjected to prolonged storage.

For iron fortification of liquid foods, such as milk, a soluble iron compound must be used to assure dispersion. Compounds that have been used successfully for iron fortification of milk include ferric ammonium citrate, ferric choline citrate and ferric glycerophosphate (Edmondson, 1969)—all iron sources with good biological availability. At least 10 mg iron per quart may be added without adversely affecting the flavor.

The iron source used for food fortification is a most important factor in availability of iron from the fortified food, even though the form may be altered by subsequent processing (Leichter and Joslyn, 1967; Theuer and others, 1970) and absorption of the iron may be modified by other diet components (Elwood and others, 1968; Layrisse and others, 1968). Several studies were made in which the relative biological values of ferrous sulfate or ferric ammonium citrate were compared when the iron salts were added directly to the test diet and when they were first incorporated into a food product, and that fortified food was then added to the test diet.

	Relative biological value of iron	
Iron Source	Ferrous sulfate	Ferric ammonium citrate
Iron salt added to test diet	100	107
Dissolved in milk	102	89
Added to biscuit mix and baked	89	..

It should be noted that in all of our studies, the iron supplement was incorporated into the diet, as it would be in any attempt to increase dietary iron by food fortification. Chelation is an important factor in utilization of food iron (Saltman, 1965), and many food constituents are powerful chelating agents. Elwood and others (1968, 1969) have questioned the efficacy of cereal enrichment and feel that the anemia problem can only be solved by supplements of medicinal iron preparations (Elwood and others, 1970). Our studies have indicated a much lesser effect from other dietary components, including eggs, other protein supplements, ascorbic acid, and small quantities of various chelating agents.

In an attempt to develop answers to questions concerning the applicability of animal test data to human utilization of iron sources, studies were made on human plasma iron responses following test doses of iron from selected iron sources. The method was essentially that described by Vellar and others (1968). The increase in plasma iron two hours after a test dose of 100 mg iron from the sample was compared to the increase following 100 mg iron from ferrous sulfate. The comparison of the data thus obtained and the relative biological values for the same samples obtained in chick and rat tests is summarized on the following page:

Iron source	Relative biological value		
	Chick Hb	Rat Hb	Human plasma iron
Ferrous sulfate	100	100	100
Ferric orthophosphate	15	16	7
Sodium iron pyrophosphate	5	15	7
Reduced iron	51	40	26
Ferrous carbonate	4	1	4

EFFICACY AND SAFETY OF FORTIFIED FOODS

It has been pointed out that, when anemia develops, the body is severely iron depleted. Very large intakes of iron are necessary to produce a rapid recovery (Fomon, 1970). This is the principal reason for claims that iron fortification of foods is not effective. The levels added might have helped to prevent iron-deficiency anemia, but they will not produce a dramatic cure after the disease has occurred (Goldsmith and others, 1970). Elwood and others (1970) point out that a minimum of 10 mg supplemental iron per day was needed to prevent a fall in hemoglobin in women who had previously been treated for anemia. Food fortification programs that furnish less than this quantity of iron cannot be expected to accomplish much in the prevention of iron-deficiency anemia.

Moe (1963) has shown that infants given cereal fortified with 12.5 mg iron per 100 grams did not develop anemia, and at one year of age had hemoglobin and hematocrit values equal to a control group that also received medicinal iron (ferrous sulfate). By contrast, groups of infants that received either unfortified cereal or cereal fortified with 5 mg iron per 100 grams did show symptoms of anemia by one year of age. The evidence is clear that enough available iron, whether given as fortified food, or as a separate supplement, will prevent iron-deficiency anemia.

Concern has been expressed by those who point out that food fortification to provide women with an average intake of 20 mg iron per day, might result in an intake of as much as 50 mg iron per day by a normal man who needs only about one-fifth of that quantity (Am. Med. Assoc., 1968). Crosby (1969) has reviewed body mechanisms that control iron absorption, and notes that the small intestine normally absorbs only as much iron as is needed to replace metabolic and other losses.

As with many other situations, the body's normal defense mechanisms can be overwhelmed by grossly excessive iron intakes. Either acute toxicity or hemosiderosis (hemochromatosis), or both, may result.

Acute iron poisoning is usually the result of ingestion of massive quantities of medicinal iron (Greengard and McEnery, 1968), and unfortunately the more available forms of iron are also the more toxic (Shanas and Boyd, 1969). Hemosiderosis may result from prolonged oral iron therapy (Johnson, 1968) but MacDonald (1970) points out that the usual cause of hemochromatosis is excessive iron intake combined with various liver disorders. A special situation exists among the Bantus where a prolonged intake of as much as 200 mg iron per day results in widespread hemosiderosis (Walker, 1956; de Bruin and others, 1970). The high iron intake is believed to come from iron vessels in which acid foods and beverages are prepared. It has long been known that such cooking utensils may contribute much to the calculated iron intake of foods (Moore, 1965), and we have found that those samples of various foods which contain much tramp iron from processing equipment tend to have higher availability of the iron than do those samples of the same foods which contain lower (inherent) iron content. Walker's comment (1956) is pertinent.

> . . . satisfactory hemoglobin levels are often maintained even in grossly malnourished pellagrins. Such observations confirm the high priority given by the body for blood production; they also suggest that, provided the iron reserves be excessively high, the other dietary hemopoietic factors are of much less importance.

A different situation involving high iron intake is seen in the Inter. Com. Nutrition Survey (1959). The very high iron intake, estimated to average about 443 mg per person per day, comes chiefly from teff. The iron present in this cereal type seed is probably much less well utilized than the more available inorganic iron compounds. The prevalence of anemia in Ethiopia is very low, despite much malnutrition and a high incidence of parasitic infection, which usually contributes to loss of iron and development of anemia (WHO, 1968).

The protection provided by the high iron Ethiopian diet is illustrated by a comparison of of the hemoglobin and hematocrit levels of pregnant women in Ethiopia (1959) and the average of comparable data for Israel, India, Mexico, and Venezeula (WHO, 1968):

Country	Hemoglobin (g/100 ml)			Hematocrit (% P.C.V.)		
	Men	Women		Men	Women	
		Non-pregnant	Pregnant		Non-pregnant	Pregnant
Ethiopia	14.4	13.2	13.2	46.6	43.3	42.3
Average of Israel, India, Mexico, and Venzuela	15.2	12.6	11.3	46.8	40.9	35.6

It is clear that the anemia of pregnancy, which is taken for granted in most of the world, does not exist in Ethiopia because of the Ethiopian high iron diet. The Ethiopian Survey (1959) also makes no mention of any problems of hemosiderosis because of continuous high iron intake.

CONCLUSIONS

The high prevalence of anemia among women and children is due chiefly to insufficient dietary iron. The situation can, and should be, corrected by increasing the iron levels in the enriched cereals, fortifying milk and other foods with iron, and by using iron sources with high biological availability for the fortification program.

REFERENCES CITED

Agricultural Research Service, 1969, Survey of food consumption of households in the United States 1965–1966: U.S. Dept. Agric. Pub. 62–18.

American Medical Association, Committee on Iron Deficiency, Council on Foods and Nutrition, 1968, Iron deficiency in the United States: Am. Med. Assoc. Jour., v. 203, p. 407–412.

Ammerman, C. B., Martin, F. G., and Arrington, L. R., 1970, Mineral contamination of feed samples by grinding: Dairy Sci. Jour., v. 53, p. 1514–1515.

Beal, V. A., 1970, Iron nutriture from infancy to adolescence: Am. Public Health Jour., v. 60, p. 666–678.

British Ministry of Health, 1968, Iron in flour: Public Health and Med. Subjects Rept., no. 117.

Code Federal Regulations, 1970, Title 21: pt. 15.10 to 16.14.

Crosby, W. H., 1969, Intestinal response to the body's requirement for iron: Am. Med. Assoc. Jour., v. 208, p. 347–351.

deBruin, E.J.P., Jansen, C. R., and Van den Berg, A. S., 1970, Iron absorption in the Bantu: Am. Dietetic Assoc. Jour., v. 57, p. 129–131.

Edmondson, L. F., 1969, Enrichment of milk with iron [ab.]: Eastern Reg. Research Lab. Collaborators Conf., Agricultural Research Service Pub. 73–67, p. 20–23.

Elwood, P. C., 1968, Iron in flour: Lancet 1968, v. 2, p. 516.

Elwood, P. C., and Waters, W. E., 1969, The vital distinction: Nutrition Today, v. 4, no. 2, p. 14–19.

Elwood, P. C., Newton, D., Eakins, J. D., and Brown, D. A., 1968, Absorption of iron from bread: Am. Clin. Nutr. Jour., v. 21, p. 1162–1169.

Elwood, P. C., Waters, W. E., and Greene, W.J.W., 1970, Evaluation of iron supplements in prevention of iron-deficiency anemia: Lancet 1970, v. 2, p. 175–177.

Federal Register, 1970, Cereal flours and related products and bakery products: Fed. Reg., v. 35, p. 5412–5413.

Fomon, S. J., 1970, Prevention of iron deficiency anemia in infants and children of preschool age: Ames, Iowa, Iowa Univ. Press.

Fritz, J. C., Pla, G. W., Roberts, T., Boehne, J. W., and Hove, E. L., 1970, Biological availability in animals of iron from common dietary sources: Agric. Food Chem. Jour., v. 18, p. 647–651.

Goldsmith, G. A., 1965, Clinical nutritional problems in the United States today: Nutr. Rev., v. 23, p. 1–3.

Goldsmith, G. A., Bradley, W. B., Finch, C. A., Moore, C. V., and White, H. S., 1970, Measures to increase iron in foods and diets: Workshop, Food and Nutr. Board Proc., Natl. Acad. Sci., Washington, D.C.

Greengard, J., and McEnery, J. T., 1968, Iron poisoning in children: Gen. Pract., v. 37, p. 88–93.

Gutelius, M. F., 1969a, The problem of iron deficiency anemia in preschool negro children: Am. Public Health Jour., v. 59, p. 290–295.

—— 1969b, Statement before the Senate Select Committee on Nutrition and Human Needs: Washington, D.C., April 15–17.

Hegsted, D. M., 1970, The recommended dietary allowances for iron: Am. Public Health Jour., v. 60, p. 653–658.

Hinton, J.J.C., and Moran, T., 1967, The addition of iron to flour. II. The absorption of reduced iron and other forms of iron by the growing rat: Food Tech. Jour., v. 2, p. 135–142.

Hofvander, Y., 1968, Hematological investigations in Ethiopia with special reference to a high iron intake: Acta Med. Scand., Suppl. 494, p. 1–74.

Höglund, S., and Reizenstein, P., 1968, Treatment of iron deficiency anemia. Enrichment of

foods and medicinal iron: Läkartidningen, v. 65, p. 5203–5206.
Interdepartmental Committee on Nutrition for National Defense, 1959, Ethiopia nutrition survey, p. 1–210.
Johnson, B. F., 1968, Hemochromatosis resulting from prolonged oral iron therapy: New England Med. Jour., v. 278, p. 1100–1101.
Layrisse, M., Martinez-Torres, C., and Roche, M., 1968, Effect of interaction of various foods on iron absorption: Am. Jour. Clin. Nutr., v. 21, p. 1175–1183.
Leichter, J., and Joslyn, M. A., 1967, The state of iron in flour, dough, and bread: Cereal Chem., v. 44, p. 346–352.
MacDonald, R. A., 1970, Hemochromatosis: a perlustration: Am. Jour. Clin. Nutr., v. 23, p. 592–603.
Moe, P. J., 1963, Iron requirements in infancy: Acta Paediat., Suppl. 150, p. 9–67.
Moore, C. V., 1965, Iron nutrition and requirements: Haematologia, v. 6, p. 1–14.
National Academy of Sciences-National Research Council, 1968a, Nutrient requirements of swine; Natl. Acad. Sci. Pub. 1599, p. 1–69.
—— 1968b, Recommended dietary allowances, 7th ed.: Natl. Acad. Sci. Pub. 1694, p. 1–101.
—— 1969, United States-Canadian tables of feed composition, 2nd revision: Natl. Acad. Sci. Pub. 1684, p. 1–92. See also publications 449 and 585.
Natvig, H., 1969, Iron in the diet: Livsmedelsteknik, no. 9, p. 469–471.
Peden, J. C., 1967, Present knowledge of iron and copper: Nutr. Rev., v. 25, p. 321–324.
Pla, G. W., and Fritz, J. C., 1970, Availability of iron: Assoc. Official Agric. Chem. Jour., v. 53, p. 791–800.
Saltman, P., 1965, The role of chelation in iron metabolism: Chem. Education Jour., v. 42, p. 682–687.
Schaefer, A. E., 1969, Malnutrition U.S.A. [ab.]: Eastern Reg. Research Lab. Collaborators Conf., Agricultural Research Service Pub. 73-67, p. 5–6.
Shanas, M. N., and Boyd, E. M., 1969, Powdered iron from 1681 to 1968: Clin. Toxemia, v. 2, p. 37–44.
Theuer, R. C., Kemmerer, K. S., Martin, W. H., Zoumas, B. L., and Sarett, H. P., 1971, Effect of processing on availability of iron salts in liquid infant formula products-experimental soy isolate formulas: Agric. Food Chem. Jour., v. 19, p. 555–558.
Thomas, J. W., 1970, Metabolism of iron and manganese: Dairy Sci. Jour., v. 53, p. 1107–1123.
Underwood, E. J., 1962, Trace elements in human and animal nutrition, 2d ed.: New York, Academic Press, p. 10–47.
Vellar, O. D., Borchgrevink, C., and Natvig, H., 1968, Iron-fortified bread. Absorption and utilization studies: Acta Med. Scand., v. 183, p. 251–256.
Walker, A.R.P., 1956, Some aspects of nutritional research in South Africa: Nutr. Rev., v. 14, p. 321–324.
Watt, B. K., Merrill, A. L., Pecot, R. K., Adams, C. F., Orr, M. L., and Miller, D. F., 1963, Composition of foods: Agric. Handbook no. 8, Washington, D.C., U.S. Govt. Printing Office, p. 6–67.
White, H. S., 1970, Iron deficiency in young women: Am. Jour. Public Health, v. 60, p. 659–665.
World Health Organization, Scientific Group, 1968, Nutritional anaemias: World Health Organization Tech. Rept. Series no. 405, p. 1–37.
Widhe, T., 1970, Iron in our diet: Livsmedelsteknik, no. 2, p. 87–88.
Zee, P., Walters, T., and Mitchell, C., 1970, Nutrition and poverty in preschool children from impoverished black families, Memphis: Am. Med. Assoc. Jour., v. 213, p. 739–742.

Manuscript Received by the Society August 16, 1971
Published in The Geological Society of America Bulletin, March, 1972.

THE GEOLOGICAL SOCIETY OF AMERICA, INC.
SPECIAL PAPER 140, 1972

Availability of Manganese and Iron to Plants and Animals

D. J. HORVATH
Animal Nutrition and Physiology, Division of Animal & Veterinary Science, West Virginia University, Morgantown, West Virginia 26506

ABSTRACT

Mn and Fe are essential to both plants and animals and are transferred successfully from the soil in all situations in which life persists. The transfer of each is subject to numerous influences and these are likely to be more important than Fe and Mn content of parent materials. At the soil:plant interface pH and Eh are dominant factors and are frequently regulated by agronomic technology.

Of the plant macronutrients used in fertilizer, P is most likely to reduce directly the availability of Fe and Mn. Because of the cost of P, however, excess applications are likely to be infrequent.

Availability of Fe and Mn of plants to animals is characteristically described as low, in the order of 10^{-1}. However, availability increases during deficiency and, in the case of Fe, following hemorrhage. The availability data reflect homeostatic mechanisms which minimize the chances of accumulation of excess Fe. Mn homeostasis appears to be largely achieved through excretory paths.

Fe deficiency is considered one of the most common trace-element deficiencies of man. Intensive agronomic practices will have little effect, however, on the Fe or Mn status of grazing animals; and, to the extent that he is a tertiary consumer in the food chain, effects on man of regional geochemical differences and changes induced by intensive agricultural technology are likely to be damped.

INTRODUCTION

Manganese (Mn) and iron (Fe) are essential elements to plants and animals; their availability is affected by other nutrient elements and other environmental factors so that deficiency or toxicity may occur as the result of such interactions.

Estimates of the concentrations of Mn and Fe in nature and of the levels recommended for beef cows are shown in Table 1, as are those of Ca and Se which have been selected for comparison. Several points will be noted: (1) the range of values reported for temperate forages in the United States is roughly one order of magnitude; (2) the generally greater mineral concentrations in legumes, represented here by alfalfa, than in grasses do not pertain to Mn; (3) the level of Fe in the open ocean has been suggested by Hutchinson (1970) as limit-

TABLE 1. COMPARISON OF LEVELS OF FOUR ELEMENTS EXPRESSED AS PPM

Element	Earth's crust*	Sea water*	Orchard grass†	Alfalfa†	Wheat (whole grain)†	Beef, lean ground, cooked (60% H_2O basis)§	Man-(70% H_2O basis)*	NRC: Cattle, recommended**
Calcium	36,000	400	5,300 (2,000-8,500)	17,200 (8,300-29,500)	600 (100-4,100)	120	15,000	2,300
Iron	50,000	0.0034	230 (70-770)	330 (250-590)	60 (10-120)	35	57	10
Manganese	1,000	0.0007-0.001	143 (38-530)	50 (28-155)	55 (0.0-86)	..	0.3#	1-10††
Selenium	0.09	0.004	..	..	..	..	present	.05-.10

* Schroeder (1965)
† Miller, D. F. (1958)
§ Watt, B. K., and Merrill, A. L. (1963)
\# Anke, M., and Groppel, B. (1970) reported 5.6 ppm Mn as the total body level in goats.
** National Research Council (1970)
†† Rojas and others (1965) recommended 20 ppm for cattle in the Pacific Northwest.

ing to marine life although earlier Redfield (1958) had deduced that P was limiting to marine photosynthesis; (4) the concentration of Mn and Fe is about 1×10^{-3} as great at the end of the food chain, man, as in the earth's crust and appears notably different from that for Se or Ca. (In the case of Ca however, if one restricts consideration to soft tissue, the overall ratio declines by 10^2.)

The changes in concentration of Mn and Fe along the food chain appear different from those of Hg, at least when that element has been methylated (Abelson, 1970), and of Se (Underwood, 1966), and of some pesticides. Hodgson (1969) compiled data for the ratio of concentration of several elements in plants compared to their concentration in soils. Cd, B, and Br had ratios greater than 1. Those for Mn and Fe were 0.065 and 0.008, respectively.

Regionally, high water or soil trace-element concentrations of Fe and Mn exist (Cannon, 1969), but they are not necessarily reflected in correspondingly high concentrations in animal tissues. One might speak of homeostatic influences on Mn and Fe in the food chain, that is, regional variations are damped rather than enhanced. This condition appears not to occur to the same degree in the case of Se. Admittedly, Underwood (1966) indicates that not all seleniferous soils are associated with selenosis in animals presumably because in some instances the Se occurs as basic iron selenide.

It is insufficient to assume that Se is not subject to homeostatic influences. Allaway and others (1968) and Kubota and others (1968) found that Se in human blood had the least variation (computed as range/mean) of any of six elements studied (Table 2). Admittedly, blood levels of a mineral are not always adequate for estimating body status of some elements, for instance Cu (Dreosti and Quicke, 1968; Todd, 1969). The effectiveness of homeostatic mechanisms will vary with the chemical form of the element. Complex formation and valence changes may have profound effects. In general, the most common oxidation state may be expected to be most readily regulated.

TABLE 2. VARIABILITY OF SELECTED ELEMENTS IN SAMPLES OF BLOOD OF HUMAN RESIDENTS OF 19 U.S. CITIES

Element	Ratio of range (max-min): mean*
Se	1.2
Zn	3.6
Cu	8.7
Cd	7.7
Pb	8.2
Mo	8.6

*Values computed from data of Allaway and others (1968) and Kubota and others (1968)

AVAILABILITY OF MN AND FE TO PLANTS

The emphasis in this section will be upon terrestrial plants grown under cultivation and upon those environmental factors more easily manipulated by practices of agronomy. Citations are intended to illustrate a given point. Moreover, the processes of conversion of crustal material to soil will not be considered because they have been reviewed previously by Mitchell (1964) and Hodgson (1969).

Apart from sandy soils and given adequate water for plant growth, the most important single variable determining availability is likely to be pH of the soil solution rather than the Mn or Fe content of the soil. Under reducing conditions both metals occur as the soluble divalent ions, and these ions are the principal form in which they are absorbed, although Sutcliffe (1962) also lists manganate ions as absorbable. However, the increased availability under acid conditions is not necessarily a direct effect of pH on the metals. Barber (1968) concluded that plants grown in sterile culture could acquire sufficient Fe from precipitated $Fe(OH)_3$ at a pH above 7, presumably by secretion of acids or complexing agents from the root hairs, or both; pH-dependent microorganisms are important intermediaries in the effects of pH on metal availability. Specifically, "grey speck" of oats (a Mn deficiency sign) is caused by oxidation of the Mn by bacterial activity. Conversely, oxidized Mn may be made available to plants by action of microbes under other conditions.

Microorganisms may hasten mineralization and produce complexes of metals which are readily available to the plants. Bloomfield (1969, personal commun.) incubated granular metal oxides with alfalfa either aerobically or anaerobically. He then dialyzed the solution collected below the sintered layer and assayed the dialysate for metal availability using pea plants. He found that Mn from anaerobic incubation was more available than that from aerobic incubation and concluded that the difference was due to formation of soluble complexes. These methods have been published by Kee and Bloomfield (1961, 1962). Also humic acids which render Fe more available may aid the growth of some plants in alkaline soils (Sutcliffe, 1962). However, complex formation has also been suggested as the cause of reduced Mn availability in acid soils of high organic matter content.

The extent of root involvement in creating reducing conditions and elaborating complexing agents was reviewed by Hodgson (1963). Soybean plants display responses that can be described as homeostatic. Roots of plants in Fe-low conditions exude strongly fluorescent compounds which did not appear when the Fe supply was adequate. Moreover, these compounds appeared in association with roots of an iron chlorosis-resistant variety, not with those of a susceptible variety.

Jones (1969) indicated that Mn and Fe deficiencies in sensitive plants are likely to occur above pH 6.3 and that chelated forms of Fe may be effective soil amendments under such circumstances. (Mn chelates have lower stability constants and are not effective except as foliar sprays.) Moreover, Browman and others (1969) found that the best determinant of plant (maize)-available Mn, based on 63 diverse U.S. soils, was a regression equation using independent variables of Mn extracted with ammonium acetate plus soil pH. The combination of these predictors accounted for 53 percent of the variability in Mn uptake by the plant. Field control of excess Mn availability through control of pH has been recognized in the problem of apple bark necrosis (Mn toxicity) which is solved by liming of the soil.

Reith (1970) reported that Mn levels (ppm) in pasture herbage from a Scottish soil varied with pH (Table 3). Mitchell (1954) set the Mn deficiency level (for plants) somewhere below 20 ppm. However, he noted that levels as high as 5,000 ppm have been reported in plants under very acid conditions. Finally, pH influences botanical composition of a pasture or range which also alters Mn and Fe levels in herbage available to the animals.

For a recent study of pH-Eh interrelations in Fe and Mn equilibria, see Collins and Buol (1970a, 1970b).

Total salt concentration influences uptake of some elements and is important in the case of

TABLE 3. CONCENTRATION OF Mn IN PASTURE HERBAGE, PPM
(Data of Reith, 1970)

Soil pH	5.0	5.5	6.0	6.5	7.0
Ryegrass	104	68	51	23	13
Clover	55	30	22	14	12

Na, K, Ca, and Mg. However, the effects of specific elements appear to be more critical for Mn and Fe. Of these the most important is phosphorus.

Formation in the soil of insoluble hydrated phosphates (Sutcliffe, 1962) would result in lowered Fe availability. Moreover

> Some ions, e.g. iron and manganese, tend to be more concentrated relative to other cations in roots than in shoots, and this is attributable to formation of insoluble inorganic salts (e.g. insoluble phosphates) or organic complexes, which render the ions unavailable for transfer into the shoot.

The effect of soil phosphate on Fe concentrations of turnip greens was noted in a southern (United States) regional study by Lucas and others (1959).

> Iron content . . . was negatively correlated with the ratio C/A (cations/anions) and especially with phosphate saturation. The mechanism governing iron absorption appears to be complex. Apparently the greater the general exchange capacity of the soil, the more conducive conditions are to iron absorption. If, however, the exchange mechanism for anions is relatively saturated with phosphate, and if the ratio, C/A, is high, iron absorption is depressed.

The correlation between leaf Fe content and soil P saturation was -0.59 ($P < 0.05$).

The adverse effect of soil phosphate (PO_4) on Zn concentration in plants is generally recognized. There is a less well-known inverse relation between soil Zn status and plant Fe concentration which is magnified when soil PO_4 is increased (Jackson and others, 1967). Moreover, application of 11 kg Zn/hectare reduced the Mn level of corn leaves sixfold in a study by Dingus and Keefer (1969) on an intensively fertilized (NPK) Monongahela silt loan soil brought to pH 6.8. This soil is characteristically low in Zn (1.3 ppm "available"). Rice also responds in growth and tissue levels to an increased Zn level in nutrient solutions when Mn is present at levels which limit growth (Ishizuka and Ando, 1968).

In addition to the effect of Zn noted above, there are other trace-element effects. Mn and Fe are mutually antagonistic under some conditions.

Fe and Mn have been shown to interact with each other in some rice culture soils. Mai-Thi and Ponnamperuma (1966) recommended the addition of MnO_2 to counteract Fe toxicity in acid sulfate soils managed for flooded rice culture. Rice in culture solution also reveals a mutual antagonism of Fe and Mn on uptake of Mn and Fe (Tanaka and Navasero, 1966).

Allaway (1968) noted that the Mn toxicity level in plants depends on the Fe:Mn ratio, and Price (1968) concluded that the physiological lesions in Fe deficiency would be caused by the decomposition, or failure of formation, of the least stable chelates in the plant and the probable replacement of Fe by Mn or other heavy metal ions. Copper can also impair Fe uptake in rice and barley grown in nutrient solutions (Dokiya and others, 1968).

Finally, chloride, as band-applied KCl, increased corn foliar Mn content when the corn was grown on poorly drained acid soils having Mn concretions (Jackson and others, 1966), whereas K as either the sulfate or the carbonate did not alter foliar Mn levels.

Nitrogen fertilization may alter plant Fe and Mn levels as the result of its ability to reduce soil pH or, conversely, to increase dry matter yield thereby possibly diluting some elements. However, when Reith (1970) used nitrochalk $Ca(NO_3)_2$ as the only N source which would limit effects due to pH, he found a consistent reduction in Mn in herbage on Scottish soils. The data in Tables 4 and 5 provide an illustration of changes in the eastern United States. Under conditions in our experiments, N generally increased both Mn and Fe. An effort was made to minimize the decrease in pH associated with intense N fertilization, but some decline did occur. The effect of P in the soil with the lowest P-fixing ability was contrary to the expected long-term effect. The increase of Fe and Mn in plants may be a short-term effect of the acidity resulting from superphosphate: pH fell to 5.4 at the higher level of P. It is worth noting, however, that root development appeared to be favored by P application, although this was not borne out by root dry-weight measurements. (The data in Table 5 are not offered as definitive, but rather as an illustration of the form in which we believe answers to these questions ought to be provided.)

TABLE 4. EFFECT OF N AND P FERTILIZATION UPON Mn AND Fe LEVELS OF SWEET CORN, PPM
(Data of Keefer and Singh, West Virginia University)

N level, kg/hectare	Soil* Monongahela Fe	Mn	Huntington Fe	Mn	Wharton Fe	Mn
0	72	56	112	21	93	35
110	111	94	86	28	89	63
220	107	109	105	37	105	83
330	115	95	101	28	129	69
	(P at 55 kg/hectare in all soils)					
P level, kg/hectare						
0	72	56	112	21	93	35
55	111	94	86	28	89	63
110	145	103	93	36	90	42
220	199	137	120	42	86	51
	(N at 110 kg/hectare in all soils)					
P level <0.05	26	16	23	15	24	3

*The soils are listed from left to right in increasing order of PO_4 fixing ability, and this is associated with the level of hydrous Al and Fe oxides or amorphous fraction of these soils. All soils were brought to pH 6.4, and a portion of the N supplied was as $Ca(NO_3)_2$ to minimize reduction of soil pH.

Table 6 provides an approximation of the removal of Mn from soil by one cropping procedure. The values are similar to those in Table 7, computed in English measurement units, for cut grass by Whitehead (1966). Return of manure would reduce these figures to the extent that liming and specific element interactions would outweigh effects of cropping.

Potassium fertilization appears to have little influence on Mn or Fe content of plants, except for one report of increased Mn levels in herbage dressed with KCl for 50 yrs (Thompson, 1957).

AVAILABILITY OF MN AND FE TO ANIMALS

Emphasis in this section will be upon grazing species and domestic livestock other than poultry. Drinking water as a source of Mn and Fe will not be considered because, except for areas of industrial or acid mine drainage pollution, levels of these elements in water, reported by Kopp and Kroner (1970), are not likely to make a major contribution to nutrition of the animal.

The literature concerning these metals is, at first glance, contradictory. "A major cause of deficiencies . . . for animals is that only a small part of the iron, manganese, or zinc contained in some plants is utilized by the animal. . . . If they were all utilized the amounts of iron, manganese, and zinc in plants would generally be adequate to meet the needs of man and animals." The foregoing summary from the U.S. Plant Soil and Nutrition Laboratory (1965) can be juxtaposed with the following from Underwood (1966).

> There is no convincing evidence that iron deficiency ever occurs in grazing stock under natural conditions, except possibly in circumstances involving severe blood loss or disturbance in iron metabolism as a consequence of parasitic infestation or disease. . . . Nutritional disabilities clearly attributable to lack of dietary manganese in stock grazing . . .

TABLE 5. PREDICTION EQUATIONS FOR TRACE-ELEMENT COMPOSITION AND YIELD OF LEAVES OF FIRST CROP OF CORN RAISED ON MONONGAHELA SOIL FOLLOWING FERTILIZATION WITH N, P, AND K
(Data of Keefer and Singh, West Virginia University)

Dependent variable = Independent variables having $P<0.01$ effect	Percent variance accounted for
Mn, ppm = $58.5 + 123.3\ P - 35.4\ P^3 - 6.17\ N^3P^{3*} + 14.0\ NP^3$	46
Fe, ppm = $63.2 + 136.0\ P - 1.61\ N^3 - 18.36\ P^3$	62
Cu, ppm = $2.5 + 7.12\ P - 2.05\ P^2 - 1.42\ NP^2 + 0.56\ NP^3$	66
Zn, ppm = $25.5 - 2.34\ P^* - 3.88\ N^2 + 1.31\ N^3$	28
Dry matter, g = $3.9 + 3.29\ N - 0.44\ N^2$	86
P, percent = $0.11 + 0.28\ P - 0.04\ N$	87
Ca, percent = $0.55 - 0.048\ N + 0.00035\ N^3P^{3*}$	26
Mg, percent = $0.33 - 0.030\ N + 0.011\ P^2 - 0.047\ PK + 0.0052\ NPK^3 - 0.00008\ N^3P^3K^3$	61
K, percent = $2.09 + 0.15\ P^* - 0.054\ N^2$	25

*$P<0.05$

manganese deficient areas have never been observed. . . .

Rojas and others (1965) have reported, however, that abnormalities observed in bones of calves in the Pacific Northwest can be duplicated by feeding cows diets having less than 20 ppm Mn.

Emphasis on limitations in availability of these elements is not merely academic. One must distinguish among animal species and physiological states. Poultry have a notably higher Mn requirement than mammals and a major ingredient of their diet is likely to be maize which is low in Mn (Underwood, 1966). Likewise, menstruating primates or suckling animals, particularly piglets and calves reared on wood or concrete floors, may develop nutritional anemia. In short, animals foraging under conditions reasonably similar to those under which they evolved are unlikely to display a deficiency of either metal although they absorb only a small fraction of the total dietary level. In fact the low availability may be in part the result of physiological absorption and transport mechanisms which also protect the animal from uptake of toxic amounts.

Having somewhat discounted the importance of availability of these metals, we shall nonetheless look at the data available on this question. Thompson's laboratory has systematically assayed forages for Fe availability using hemoglobin regeneration in young anemic rats and comparing responses to ferric chloride as 100 percent (Table 8). All diets provided 0.2 mg Fe/day. In every instance, $FeCl_3$ was superior to the Fe in the plant material: in general about twice as available. Presumably, ferrous salts would have been even better (Fritz, 1969). While not assayed with grazing species of animals, the data are useful as an indication of the problems of availability. The extent to which organic complexes (for example, phytate, citrate, or malate) are responsible for this effect is not known. In the case of Mn however, Bremner and Knight (1970) concluded that the soluble Mn in rye grass ". . . was present only in the cationic and probably noncomplexed form." (Complex formation was predominant

TABLE 6. MANGANESE TRANSFER IN A HYPOTHETICAL ECOSYSTEM

	Total soil Mn, ppm (63 U.S. soils)*	Ammon Acetate available Mn, ppm (63 U.S. soils)*	Calc. total Mn in plow layer, kg/hectare	Expected maize Mn content, ppm†	Expected yield of maize silage, kilo tons/hectare	Calc. Mn removal per year kg/hectare§	Calc. Mn removal if all cattle manure returned to land, kg/hectare#
Means	753	6.4	845	68	28	1.9	<0.03
Extremes	30-2,500	0.2-98	66-2,800	5-82 (23 observations)		0.14-2.3	

* Browman and others (1969)
† Miller, D. F., 1958, p. 361
§ assumes no difference in yield
# assumes beef cattle finished from 230 to 460 kg principally on corn silage and having a mean tissue Mn level of 2 ppm or a total removal of .46 g/head x 20 head/hectare = 9.2 g Mn. Anke and Groppel (1970) reported 5.6 ppm Mn in bodies of goats. If this were the case for cattle, the total would still be less than 30 g/hectare.

TABLE 7. MINERAL REMOVAL BY HARVESTED GRASS (Whitehead, 1966)

	Low yield: 5,000 lb DM/A		High yield: 10,000 lb DM/A	
	Assumed content	Removal/ yr/A	Assumed content	Removal/ yr/A
Fe	100 ppm	8 oz	300 ppm	3 lb
Mn	20 ppm	1.6 oz	200 ppm	2 lb
Ca	0.5 %	25 lb	1.5 %	150 lb
Se	0.1 ppm	0.008 oz	1 ppm	0.16 oz

in the case of the soluble Zn and Cu in the same study and both were said to be present only in the anionic form.) Unfortunately, this evidence concerning the form of metal in foodstuffs does not preclude the possibility of alteration of form in the various portions of the gut as will be reviewed below. It is now believed that both Mn and Fe are absorbed in the 2^{+} valence state and transported in the 3^{+} state (Sandstead, 1967; Frieden, 1970).

Mn

Cotzias (1960) in reviewing the functions of Mn, indicated that a wide Ca:P ratio aggravates Mn deficiency. Phosphates and carbonates may interfere through adsorption of Mn by solid mineral in the gut (Underwood, 1966).

Susceptibility to Mn deficiency varies among different strains of poultry. Also a marked difference is seen in the "pallid" mouse, which develops ataxia unless the dam's diet contains 1,000 ppm Mn during midgestation. Cotzias (1967) outlined the aspects of the pallid-mouse condition that suggested that the problem might be one of absorption. However, Hurley (1968) reported that the defect occurred in the matrix in which otoliths are formed rather than in absorption from the gut.

Regulation of Mn absorption due to availability of a specific Mn transport globulin, transmanganin, may not be the only control of net Mn absorption. Bertinchamps and Cotzias (*in* Cotzias, 1960) found that biliary excretion of injected labelled Mn was affected by the amount of Mn in the diet and that two pathways of Mn excretion may exist based on the occurrence of two peaks in the time course of injected labelled Mn concentration in bile. Excretion appears to be the principal Mn homeostatic process.

TABLE 8. GAINS IN TOTAL HEMOGLOBIN PERCENT OF $FeCl_3$ RESPONSE

	Species	ppm Fe	Per-cent	
Grasses*	Perennial ryegrass	242	50	
	Orchardgrass	95	48	
	Timothy	128	63	(P<0.01 *versus* other grasses)
Clovers†	Alsike	523	57	
	Broad red	755	55	
	Kent wild white	718	47	(P<0.05 *versus* Alsike)
	Alfalfa	856	51	
Herbs§	Burnet	299	39	
	Chicory	621	50	
	Narrow leaved plantain	442	55	(P<0.05 *versus* Burnet)

* Thompson and Raven (1959)
† Raven and Thompson (1959)
§ Raven and Thompson (1961)

Competition of other metals in Mn absorption by isolated perfused rat intestinal loops has been reported by Sahagian and others (1967). They found that Zn, Cd, Hg, and Mn were competitive with regard to mucosal uptake (binding), but that uptake was not dependent on expenditure of metabolic energy, nor did it occur against a concentration difference, nor was it unidirectional. Although the competition suggests a common site for binding, there was, on the other hand, no apparent competition in transport between the two essential metals Zn and Mn. The transport of Mn from the mucosa to serosa was greatly enhanced by Cd (or EDTA), but depressed by Hg.

Fe inhibited Mn absorption, and vice versa, in the digestion studies of Forth (1970) using 10^2 ratios of competitor in rat intestinal loops. It must be remembered that presence of dietary proteins and carbohydrates might have altered these relationships, as in the case of Cu in the intact animal (Kirchgessner and Grassman, 1970).

The changes in availability of Mn in ingesta from a dried grass ration have been studied by Bremner (1970). In the rumen only 5 to 10 percent of the Mn was available, and he suggested association of the metal with microbial matter. Solubility increased tenfold in the acid abomasum (50 to 80 percent), and the Mn was apparently in noncomplexed form. In the small intestine, solubility decreased linearly to about 50 percent at the junction of the jejunum and ileum and then increased again, partly due to changes in pH. Perhaps bile influence will be found to exist, judging from the observations of Cotzias (1960).

Fe

Iron availability is reduced by dietary phosphate and phytate, presumably by formation of insoluble ferric phosphate and phytate (Underwood, 1966). Most feedstuff-Fe is in the ferric form in organic combinations; the normal absorption is from 5 to 10 percent of food iron in healthy simple-stomached animals, but is 40 to 60 percent in deficient animals (Underwood, 1966), suggesting that availability is largely host regulated. Data for availability to herbivores are lacking, but Fleming (1965) among others has pointed out that often much of the Fe ingested by grazing animals results from soil particles clinging to the forage. Presumably a large portion of such Fe would be in the ferric state.

Mn absorption increases in Fe deficiency induced either by bleeding or by an Fe-deficient diet (Pollack and others, 1965), suggesting competition in absorptive pathways.

The concept of mucosal block of Fe absorption has been discounted by some workers (Peden, 1967) insofar as apoferritin's role is concerned. In experimental iron loading or in Cu deficiency, tissue Fe accumulation does occur, although the process is presumably more gradual than would be the case in the absence of specific transport mechanisms. The distinction between mucosal block and (rate limiting) transport is equivalent to that made by Sahagian and others (1967) for Mn absorption and transport. However, Forth (1970) further refined the absorption concept referring to an Fe-binding system for the upper small intestine based on in vitro data and data from ligated loops in vivo. Forth distinguishes among (1) penetration of the mucosa by ^{59}Fe, (2) binding of ^{59}Fe in the mucosal cell, and (3) transport of ^{59}Fe. The competition for absorption noted in his studies is greatest for metals, such as Co and Ni, which are not likely to be present in the diet at levels comparable to that of Fe.

The recent data of Kaufman and others (1966) support absorption as the principal homeostatic regulator of Fe in the rat. After 4 days on an Fe-deficient diet, Fe absorption increased abruptly. Moreover, from data obtained by bleeding, they concluded that neither the liver Fe pool nor the pool at the sites of erythropoiesis were important regulators of Fe absorption. (In man after 13 days on an Fe deficient diet, no such absorptive response had occurred.)

Callender (1966) reviewed evidence indicating a role of pancreatic secretions in modifying Fe absorption.

FIELD PROBLEMS ASSOCIATED WITH MN AND FE IN GRAZING SPECIES

Manganese deficiency in animals on soils low in available Mn is virtually unknown. There are, however, several reports of Mn responsive conditions in cattle in Britain and Holland, reviewed by Underwood (1966). In the United States, bone abnormalities in beef calves in Washington have been associated with low Mn diets of the dam by Rojas and others (1965). In addition, Bourne (1967) has a note on a similar field problem, and Thornton and Webb (1970) reported low Mn levels in stream sediment in the area of low Mn and infertility in Britain. However, Hartmans (1970) stated that the reports of conditioned Mn deficiency from the Netherlands were re-examined carefully and could not be confirmed. Conversely, excess Mn is not often a problem in animals, although Mn levels of cows' milk increase up to twofold with increasing dietary Mn (Underwood, 1966).

Iron deficiency is also rare in grazing animals in the absence of disease or parasites. One report from New Zealand of disorders of cattle grazing pasture contaminated with irrigation water rich in $Fe(OH)_3$ was noted by Whitehead (1966).

INFLUENCE OF INTENSIFICATION OF AGRONOMIC INPUTS, SPECIFICALLY NPK, ON ANIMALS

Though little influence of NPK upon animal responses is likely to occur by way of effects on Fe and Mn in grazing species, the general subject is of sufficient interest to permit me to exceed the limits of the title of this paper. Early studies of this question were at NPK levels which are now regularly exceeded. Perhaps for this reason, no obvious changes in animal health or metabolism were noted. The only general trend emerging in practice is the increased incidence of hypomagnesemic tetany in cattle in association with intensive N and K applications (Kemp, 1958; Horvath, 1959). Despite this, the staff of the U.S. Plant, Soil, and Nutrition Laboratory properly concluded (1965) that quite often fertilized crops were slightly superior to the unfertilized one. The differences were greater if the fertilizer included Co on a Co-deficient soil. The increase in yield, which motivates the producer to apply increased levels of N, is often accompanied by an increase in protein content which would also increase the nutritive value of the crop.

The possibility exists that more intensive macronutrient inputs will alter microelement levels or availability, or both, sufficiently to influence animal health. This premise has been tested at West Virginia for the past 4 years. Briefly, iodine metabolism was altered in sheep

TABLE 9. EFFECT OF N FERTILIZATION OF HAY UPON THYROIDS OF RATS FED 40 PERCENT ORCHARDGRASS DIETS. MEANS OF 3 LEVELS OF I IN EACH VALUE*

	High N Hay	Low N Hay	Control Diet
Cell height, μ	5.7	4.9	3.8
Gland wt. mg. (adjusted for body wt.)	22.0	19.0	16.7
Percent ^{131}I dose present in gland at 24 hr (adjusted for gland wt)	22	23	16

* Data of Lee and others (1970). Each value in each row is different (P<0.05) from each other value.

(Reid and others, 1969b; Horn, 1970) and rats (Lee and others, 1970) with intensive (450 kg/hectare) N fertilization of orchardgrass (Table 9). (This level of N would not be considered excessive in Britain and Holland where rates up to 660 kg/hectare are considered feasible.) Calcium balance of lactating goats was favorably affected (Daniel and others, 1969) which is not in agreement with the lowered Ca availability and negative Ca balance of cows reported by Mudd (1970) with either K or NK combined. However, Mg balance in the goats was adversely affected. Studies in progress (Reid and others, unpub. data) indicate that both Cu and Zn status may be altered. In a separate experiment (Reid and others, 1969a), Zn fertilizer consistently increased dry matter digestibility of the forage, and Singh and Keefer (1968) have shown that P fertilization of some soils leads to plant Zn levels as low as 10 ppm, which would be expected to be a deficient ration for animals. To date no evidence of effects of NPK on Fe and Mn status of animals have been revealed in our studies.

The addition of phosphorus fertilizer with or without lime to a low P status Florida soil had no effect upon hemoglobin values of grazing cows (Kirk and others, 1970). Levels were of the order of 50 lb P_2O_5/A for 20 yrs.

For a broader review of agronomic controls of trace element cycling, see Allaway (1968). Estimates of changes in elemental concentrations from soil to plant and plant to animal are presented in Table 10.

CONCLUSIONS

The most important single variable controlling availability of Mn and Fe to plants is soil pH, but specific elemental interactions also occur, notably that of P with Mn and Fe. Despite the impact of these variables on plant growth, the availability of Mn and Fe to normal grazing animals although low (approximately 10 percent) is of limited importance. Further, geochemical differences in these two elements tend to be damped toward the end of the food chain. The relative magnitude of regulation of transfer of both Mn and Fe in the food chain appears to be 10^{-1} at the plant:animal interface (net availability of dietary Mn and Fe) and 10^{-2} at the soil:plant interface

TABLE 10. TRANSFER OF ELEMENTS ALONG THE FOOD CHAIN INCLUDING ORDER OF MAGNITUDE APPROXIMATIONS OF CHANGE IN CONCENTRATION

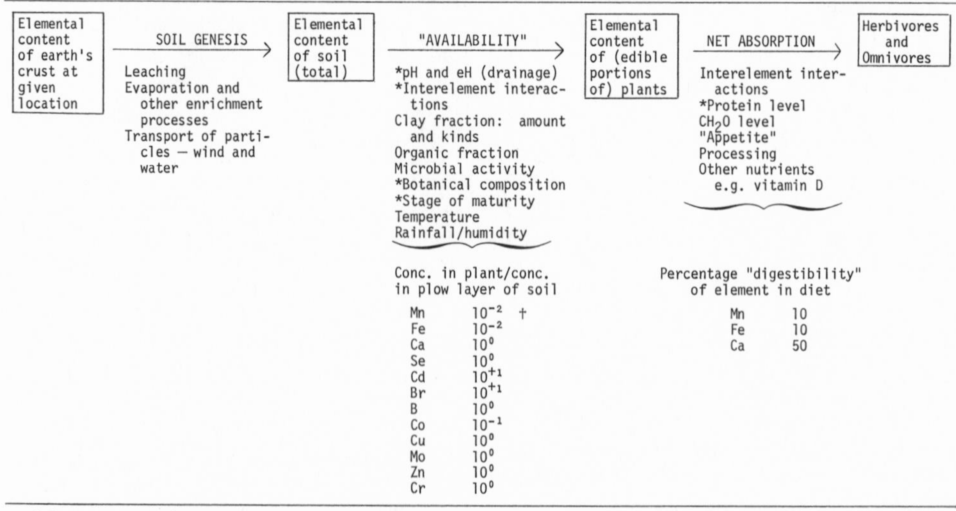

* Factors relatively easy to control by agronomic practices
† Data adapted from various sources, principally Hodgson (1969)

when one compares concentrations in the various phases.

In the case of Fe, homeostatic mechanisms are apparent in some species of organisms at both interfaces. The principal homeostatic regulators in animals for Mn and Fe are excretion and absorption, respectively. In examining plants and animals for evidence of homeostatic regulation of various trace elements, the valence state and existence of complexes of the elements emerge as major considerations. Likewise, short-term studies must be viewed cautiously.

As man alters the environment of animals, as by rearing them in confinement, or on diets composed largely of milk or seeds, or both, the level and availability of these two elements become critical.

The increased use of NPK fertilizers does not appear to cause major changes in movement of Mn and Fe from plants to animals if pH is also regulated.

REFERENCES CITED

Abelson, P. H., 1970, Methyl mercury: Science, v. 169, p. 237.

Allaway, W. H., 1968, Agronomic controls over the environmental cycling of trace elements: Advances in Agronomy, v. 20, p. 235.

Allaway, W. H., Kubota, J., Losee, F., and Roth, M., 1968, Selenium, molybdenum and vanadium in human blood: Arch. Environ. Health, v. 16, p. 342.

Anke, M., and Groppel, B., 1970, Manganese deficiency and radioisotope studies on manganese metabolism, *in* Mills, C. F., ed., TEMA Symp. Aberdeen, 1969 Proc.: Edinburgh & London, E. & S. Livingstone, p. 133.

Barber, D. A., 1968, Microorganisms and the inorganic nutrition of higher plants: Ann. Rev. Plant Phys., v. 19, p. 71.

Bourne, F. J., 1967, Manganese: Its relationship to infertility in the bovine: Feed Forum, v. 2, p. 33.

Bremner, F. J., 1970, The nature of trace element binding in herbage and gut contents, *in* Mills, C. F., ed., TEMA Symp. Aberdeen, 1969 Proc.: Edinburgh & London, E. & S. Livingstone, p. 366.

Bremner, I., and Knight, A. H., 1970, The complexes of zinc, copper and manganese present in ryegrass: British Jour. Nutrition, v. 24, p. 279.

Browman, M. G., Chesters, G., and Pionke, H. B., 1969, Evaluation of tests for predicting the availability of soil manganese to plants: Jour. Agric. Sci., v. 72, p. 335.

Callender, Shelia T., 1966, Iron absorption: Nutrition Soc. Proc., v. 26, p. 59.

Cannon, Helen L., 1969, Trace element excesses and deficiencies in some geochemical provinces of the U.S.: 3d Ann. Conf. Trace Substances in Environ. Health, Univ. Missouri, Columbia, Missouri.

Collins, J. F., and Buol, S. W., 1970a, Effects of fluctuations in the Eh-pH environment on iron and/or manganese equilibria: Soil Sci., v. 110, p. 111.

—— 1970b, Patterns of iron and manganese precipitation under specified Eh-pH conditions: Soil Sci., v. 110, p. 157.

Cotzias, G. C., 1960, Metabolic relations of manganese to other minerals: Fed. Proc., v. 19, p. 655.

—— 1967, Importance of trace substances in environmental health as exemplified by manganese: 1st Ann. Conf. on Trace Substances in Environ. Health, Univ. Missouri, Columbia, Missouri.

Daniel, K., Reid, R. L., and Jung, G. A., 1969, Mineral balance of lactating goats on fertilized hays [abs.]: Jour. Animal Sci., v. 29, p. 179.

Dingus, D. D., and Keefer, R. F., 1969, Effect of interrelations among the elements Zn, Cu, Mn and Mg on the growth and composition of corn (*Zea mays L.*): West Virginia Acad. Sci. Proc., v. 40, p. 12.

Dokiya, Y., Owa, N., and Mutsui, S., 1968, Comparative physiological study of iron, manganese and copper absorption by plants. 3. Interaction of Fe, Mn and Cu on the absorption of the elements by rice and barley seedlings: Soil Sci. and Plant Nutrition, v. 14, p. 169.

Dreosti, I. E., and Quicke, G. V., 1968, Blood copper as an indicator of copper status with a note on serum proteins and leucocyte counts in copper-deficient rats: British Jour. Nutrition, v. 22, p. 1.

Fleming, G. A., 1965, Trace elements in plants with particular reference to pasture species: Outlook on Agriculture, v. 4, p. 270.

Forth, W., 1970, Absorption of iron and chemically related metals in vitro and in vivo; the specificity of an iron binding system in the intestinal mucosa of the rat, *in* Mills, C. F., ed., TEMA Symp. Aberdeen, 1969 Proc.: Edinburgh & London, E. & S. Livingstone, p. 298.

Freiden, E., 1970, Ceruloplasmin, a link between copper and iron metabolism: Nutrition Rev., v. 28, p. 87.

Fritz, J. C., 1969, Availability of iron from sources used for food and feed enrichment: Fed. Proc., v. 28, p. 692.

Hartmans, J., 1970, Influence of manganese on skeletal development in the sheep and rat [disc.]: *in* Mills, C. F., ed., TEMA Symp.

Aberdeen, 1969 Proc.: Edinburgh & London, E. & S. Livingstone, p. 130.
Hodgson, J. F., 1963, Chemistry of the micronutrient elements in soils: Advances in Agronomy, v. 15, p. 119.
—— 1969, Chemistry of trace elements in soils with reference to trace element concentration in plants: 3d Ann. Conf. Trace Substances in Environ. Health, Univ. Missouri, Columbia, Missouri.
Horn, F. P., 1970, Iodine nutrition and metabolism in grazing sheep [Ph.D. dissert.]: Morgantown, West Virginia Univ.
Horvath, D. J., 1959, Magnesium and agriculture, a symposium: Morgantown, West Virginia Univ.
Hurley, Lucille S., 1968, Genetic-nutritional interactions concerning manganese: 2d Ann. Conf. on Trace Substances in Environ. Health Proc., Univ. Missouri, Columbia, Missouri.
Hutchinson, G. E., 1970, The Biosphere: Sci. American, v. 223, p. 45.
Ishizuka, Y., and Ando, T., 1968, Interaction between manganese and zinc in growth of rice plants: Soil Sci. and Plant Nutrition, v. 14, p. 20.
Jackson, T. L., Westermann, D. T., and Moore, D. P., 1966, The effect of chloride and lime on the manganese uptake by bush beans and sweet corn: Soil Sci. Soc. America Proc., v. 30, p. 70.
Jackson, T. L., Hay, J., and Moore, D. P., 1967, The effect of Zn on yield and chemical composition of sweet corn in the Williamette Valley: Am. Soc. Hortic. Sci. Proc., v. 91, p. 462.
Jones, U. S., 1969, Food producing minerals and chemicals: South Carolina Agric. Exp. Stn. Agronomy and Soils Research Series, no. 82.
Kaufman, R. M., Pollack, S., and Crosby, W. H., 1966, Iron-deficient diet: Effects in rats and humans: Blood, v. 28, p. 726.
Kee, N. S., and Bloomfield, C., 1961, The solution of some minor element oxides by decomposing plant materials: Geochim. et Cosmochim. Acta, v. 24, p. 206.
—— 1962, The effect of flooding and aeration on the mobility of certain trace elements in soils: Plant & Soil, v. 16, p. 108.
Kemp, A., 1958, Influence of fertilizer treatment of grassland on the incidence of hypomagnesaemia and hypomagnesaemic tetany (grass tetany) in milking cows: Netherlands Jour. Agric. Sci., v. 6, p. 281.
Kirchgessner, M., and Grassman, E., 1970, The dynamics of copper absorption, *in* Mills, C. F., ed., TEMA Symp. Aberdeen, 1969 Proc.: Edinburgh & London, E. & S. Livingstone, p. 277.
Kirk, W. G., Shirley, R. L., Hodges, E. M., Davis, G. K., Peacock, F. M., Easley, J. F., and Martin, F. G., 1970, Production performance and blood and bone composition of cows grazing pangolagrass pastures receiving different phosphate fertilizers: Florida Agric. Survey Bull. 735.
Kopp, J. F., and Kroner, R. C., 1970, Trace metals in waters of the United States: U.S. Dept. Interior, Fed. Water Pollution Control Adm., Cincinnati.
Kubota, J., Lazar, V. A., and Losee, F., 1968, Copper, zinc, cadmium and lead in human blood from 19 locations in the United States: Arch. Environ. Health, v. 16, p. 788.
Lee, C., Weiss, R., and Horvath, D. J., 1970, Effects of nitrogen fertilization on the thyroid function of rats fed 40% orchardgrass diets: Jour. Nutrition, v. 100, p. 1121.
Lucas, H. L., and others, 1959, Influence of environment on the chemical composition of plants. 3. Relations of the composition of turnip greens to soil and weather factors: Southern Coop. Series Bull. 52.
Mai-Thi, My Nhung, and Ponnamperuma, F. N., 1966, Effects of calcium carbonate, manganese dioxide, ferric hydroxide and prolonged flooding on chemical and electrochemical changes and growth of rice in a flooded acid sulfate soil: Soil Sci., v. 102, p. 29.
Miller, D. F., ed., 1958, Composition of cereal grains and forages: National Research Council, Pub. 585, p. 232, 279, 327.
Mitchell, R. L., 1954, Trace elements and liming: Scottish Agric., v. 34, p. 139.
—— 1964, Trace elements in soils, *in* Bear, F. E., ed., Chemistry of the soil, 2d ed.: Am. Chem. Soc. Mon., New York, Reinhold, p. 320.
Mudd, A. J., 1970, The influence of heavily fertilized grass on mineral metabolism of dairy cows: Jour. Agric. Sci., v. 74, p. 11.
National Research Council, 1970, Nutrient requirements of domestic animals. 4. Nutrient requirements of beef cattle: Washington, D.C.
Peden, J. C., Jr., 1967, Present knowledge of iron and copper, *in* Present knowledge in nutrition, 3d ed.: New York, The Nutrition Foundation, Inc., p. 126.
Pollack, S., George, J. N., Reba, R. C., Kaufman, R. M., and Crosby, W. H., 1965, The absorption of nonferrous metals in iron deficiency: Jour. Clin. Invest., v. 44, p. 1470.
Price, C. A., 1968, Iron compounds and plant nutrition: Ann. Rev. Plant Phys., v. 19, p. 239.
Raven, A. M., and Thompson, A., 1959, The availability of iron in certain grass, clover and herb species. Pt. II. Alsike, broad clover, Kent wild white clover, trefoil and lucerne: Jour. Agric. Sci., v. 53, p. 224.
—— 1961, The availability of iron in certain grass, clover and herb species. III. Burnet, chicory and narrow-leaved plantain: Jour. Agric. Sci., v. 56, p. 229.
Redfield, A. C., 1958, The biological control of

chemical factors in the environment, *in* Kormondy, E. J., ed., Readings in ecology: New York, Prentice Hall Inc., p. 196.

Reid, R. L., Jung, G. A., and Post, A. J., 1969a, Effects of micro-element fertility on nutritive quality of orchardgrass [abs.]: Jour. Animal Sci., v. 29, p. 181.

Reid, R. L., Jung, G. A., Weiss, R., Post, A. J., Horn, F. P., Kahle, E. B., and Carlson, C. E., 1969b, Performance of ewes on nitrogen fertilized orchardgrass pastures [abs.]: Jour. Animal Sci., v. 29, p. 181.

Reith, J.W.S., 1970, Soil factors influencing the trace element content of herbage, *in* Mills, C. F., ed., TEMA Symp. Aberdeen, 1969 Proc.: Edinburgh & London, E. & S. Livingstone, p. 410.

Rojas, M. A., Dyer, I. A., and Cassatt, W. A., 1965, Manganese deficiency in the bovine: Jour. Animal Sci., v. 24, p. 664.

Sahagian, B. M., Harding-Barlow, I., and Perry, H. M., Jr., 1967, Transmural movements of zinc, manganese, cadmium and mercury by rat small intestine: Jour. Nutrition, v. 93, p. 291.

Sandstead, H. H., 1967, Present knowledge of the minerals, *in* Present knowledge in nutrition, 3d ed.: New York, The Nutrition Foundation, Inc., p. 117.

Schroeder, H. A., 1965, The biological trace elements or peripatetics through the periodic table: Jour. Chron. Dis., v. 18, p. 217.

Singh, R. N., and Keefer, R. F., 1968, Influence of heavy N, P and K application on yield and composition of crops: I. Orchardgrass [abs.]: Am. Soc. Agronomy, Northeast Mtg., p. 6.

Sutcliffe, J. F., 1962, Mineral salts absorption in plants: New York, Pergamon Press.

Tanaka, A., and Navasero, S. A., 1966, Interaction between iron and manganese in the rice plant: Soil Sci. and Plant Nutrition, v. 12, p. 29.

Thompson, A., 1957, The trace-element contents of herbage plants with some reference to their availability to the animals: Jour. Sci. of Food Agric., v. 8, p. 72.

Thompson, A., and Raven, A. M., 1959, The availability of iron in certain grass, clover and herb species: I. Perennial ryegrass, cocksfoot and timothy: Jour. Agric. Sci., v. 52, p. 177.

Thornton, I., and Webb, J. S., 1970, Geochemical reconnaissance and the detection of trace element disorders in animals, *in* Mills, C. F., ed., TEMA Symp. Aberdeen, 1969 Proc.: Edinburgh & London, E. & S. Livingstone, p. 397.

Todd, J. R., 1969, Chronic copper toxicity of ruminants: Nutrition Soc. Proc., v. 28, p. 189.

Underwood, E. J., 1966, The mineral nutrition of livestock: Food and Agriculture Organization of the United Nations and the Commonwealth Agric. Bureau, Farnham Royal, Bucks, England.

U.S. Plant, Soil, and Nutrition Laboratory, 1965, The effect of soil and fertilizers on the nutritional quality of plants: Agric. Inf. Bull. 299.

Watt, B. K., and Merrill, A. L., 1963, Composition of foods: U.S. Dept. Agriculture Handbook, no. 8, p. 15.

Whitehead, D. C., 1966, Nutrient minerals in grassland herbage: Commonwealth Bur. Pastures and Field Crops, Mimeo Pub. 1/1966, Hurley Berks, England.

Manuscript Received by the Society August 16, 1971

Published in The Geological Society of America Bulletin, February, 1972.

PRINTED IN U.S.A.

The Geological Society of America, Inc.
Special Paper 140, 1972

Selenium Accumulation in Soils and Its Absorption by Plants and Animals

Hubert W. Lakin
U.S. Geological Survey, Denver, Colorado 80225

ABSTRACT

Soils producing crop plants that are toxic because of selenium are confined to small areas, but occur throughout the world. Such soils are confined to semiarid regions or areas of impeded drainage. They contribute no significant hazard to human health and only locally to animal health.

Environmental contamination with selenium is increasing, but will probably stay well below a hazardous concentration. Locally, mining and industrial wastes may produce minor hazards. However, the effect of added selenium in the atmosphere and waters in combination with other contaminants is not known and should be studied.

INTRODUCTION

Selenium is a Doctor Jekyll and Mr. Hyde. In very low concentrations (parts per billion) it is beneficial in the diet of animals. In concentrations of only a few parts per million it is toxic in the diet. The Mr. Hyde aspect of selenium was studied in the Western United States during the decade of the 1930's when otherwise normal farm crops were found to cause chronic and often fatal poisoning of farm animals because of their selenium content. In 1957 the Doctor Jekyll aspect of selenium was discovered by Dr. Klaus Schwarz (Schwarz and Foltz, 1957); the interrelations of selenium and vitamin E are a matter of much current research.

The abundance of selenium in the earth's crust is shown in Table 1 to be 0.09 ppm—1/6,000 of the abundance of sulfur and 1/50 of the abundance of arsenic. In lunar materials that have been analyzed, selenium ranges from 0.14 to 0.25 ppm (Ganapathy and others, 1970). Selenium is detectable in most earth materials and is frequently enriched in black shales in concentrations ranging to 675 ppm. It is associated with ore deposits of uranium that are concentrated in carbonaceous debris in sandstones. Selenium is enriched in phosphate rocks (< 0.8–55 ppm Se) and accompanies phosphate fertilizers into the soil.

The geochemistry of selenium resembles, in part, that of sulfur. Selenide ions substitute for sulfide ions in the major sulfide minerals of ore deposits; consequently, selenium is sometimes emitted from smokestacks of smelters. Hydrogen selenide, selenium, and selenium dioxide accompany hydrogen sulfide, sulfur, and sulfur dioxide in volcanism; it has been estimated that volcanism has added 475 g of sulfur and 0.1 g of selenium to each square centimeter of the earth's surface (Rankama and Sahama, 1950). Selenium is present in coal and petroleum—the burning of these fuels can add selenium to the atmosphere (Hashimoto and others, 1970).

In the weathering processes selenium becomes a resistate, remaining as elemental selenium or, more frequently, as a basic ferric selenite of variable composition. In the weathering of seleniferous iron sulfides in shales, the sulfur is oxidized to sulfate and moves downward in aqueous solution. The selenium is entrapped in the ferric oxide residuum.

I shall present first a viewpoint on the chemical forms of selenium in soils as controlled by the nature of the soils; second, the variation in selenium uptake by plants with species and season; third, the toxicity of selenium to animals; and finally, the dispersion of selenium in our environment.

TABLE 1. SELENIUM CONTENT OF VARIOUS EARTH MATERIALS

Material	Selenium content (ppm)	Reference
Earth's crust	0.09	Goldschmidt (1954)
Igneous rocks	0.05	Turekian & Wedepohl (1961)
Shales	0.6	do.
Sandstones	0.05	do.
Carbonates	0.08	do.
Deep-sea sediments	0.17	do.
Soils	0.1-2	Swaine (1955)
	0.01	Vinogradov (1959)

NATURE OF TOXIC SELENIFEROUS SOILS

Vegetation containing toxic quantities of selenium is found growing in soils containing at least a few tenths of a part per million of water-soluble selenium. Such water-soluble selenium has been identified repeatedly as the selenate form in soils in midwestern United States by Williams and Byers (1936), in South Dakota soils by Olson and others (1942), and Abu-Erreish and others (1968), in Wyoming soils by Rosenfeld and Beath (1964), in soils of Ireland by Fleming and Walsh (1957), and in soils of Israel by Ravikovitch and Margolin (1957a, b).

Many, if not most, of the soils of the world do not contain measurable water-soluble selenium and do not produce vegetation that because of its selenium content is injurious to animals. Soils of Puerto Rico that contain 1 to 10 ppm selenium do not produce seleniferous vegetation (Roberts and party, 1942), nor do Hawaiian soils that contain 6 to 15 ppm selenium (Byers and others, 1938). In contrast, soils of South Dakota (Olson and others, 1942) and of Israel (Ravikovitch and Margolin, 1957a) with a lower total selenium content produce toxic vegetation.

An illustration of the lack of correlation of total selenium content of soils with the selenium content of vegetation growing in the soils is provided by seven Danish soils (Table 2). A silty clay loam containing 0.16 ppm selenium produced vegetation more seleniferous than vegetation grown in a muck containing 10 times as much selenium. Incidentally, the last soil listed in Table 2 had received 200 kg of superphosphate per hectare per year since 1942. Gregers-Hansen (1967) found 5 ppm selenium in the superphosphate. It obviously had no discernible effect on this loamy sand.

INORGANIC CHEMISTRY OF SELENIUM IN SOILS

It is evident that the form of selenium in the soil is the key to its availability to plants and subsequently to animals. The need for minute amounts of selenium in livestock diets and the hazard arising from excessive amounts pose a problem in soil management. Recent research on the availability and stability of different forms of selenium applied to low-selenium soils has yielded a much better understanding of the soil chemistry of selenium. Especially helpful in elucidating the chemistry of selenium in the soil-plant-animal relationship has been the work of W. J. Hartley in Australia, O. H. Muth and J. E. Oldfield in Oregon, and W. H. Allaway and his associates in the U.S. Plant Soil and Nutrition Laboratory at Ithaca, New York. A paper by Geering and others, (1968) presents a theoretical study of the four oxidation states of selenium as they are affected by the redox potential, soil *p*H, and ions with which selenium combines.

A guide to the probable oxidation state of selenium in equilibrium with a given environment is provided in Figure 1 by Geering and his colleagues, (1968) who plotted the oxidation potential (vertical axis) at varying *p*H (horizontal axis) for selenium ions at concentrations of 10^{-7} mol/l. This diagram shows the equilibrium valence state, but offers no assurance that equilibrium with the environment actually exists. These authors stated that the rates of transformation of SeO_3^{2-} to SeO_4^{2-} and the reverse reaction are relatively sluggish. They also studied the solution of Se^0 in soils and concluded that red amorphous Se^0 is slowly oxidized to selenite (SeO_3^{2-}), and in submerged soils Se^0 may be reduced to the selenide (Se^{2-}). Selenite is, therefore, the most likely oxidation state in soils.

Geering and his associates examined ferric

TABLE 2. SELENIUM CONTENT OF SEVEN DANISH SOILS AND OF VEGETATION GROWN IN THEM (Gregers-Hansen, 1967)

Soil type	pH (H_2O)	Organic matter (percent)	Selenium (ppm)	Selenium (ppm) in dry plant matter		
				Rye grass	Red clover	White mustard
Silty clay loam	6.8	1.7	0.16	0.4	0.20	0.5
Sandy loam	6.5	2.1	0.24	0.2	0.07	0.13
do.	6.9	2.2	0.34	0.06	0.04	0.05
Muck	7.1	13.4	1.5	0.24	0.17	0.33
Loamy sand	6.8	2.2	0.19	0.06	..	..
do.	5.8	1.7	0.30	0.08	0.03	0.07
do.	5.9	1.9	0.18	0.07	0.05	0.05

selenite (solubility product $X \cdot 10^{-33}$) and $Fe_2(OH)_4SeO_3$ (solubility product $X \cdot 10^{-62.7}$) as possible insoluble selenites in soils. They concluded that their data favored the existence of a basic ferric selenite.

Plotnikov and Kochetkov (1967) determined the distribution of selenite ions between solution and precipitated metal hydroxides from selenite solutions and the same distribution when selenite solutions were poured on freshly precipitated hydroxides. After 360 hrs they found the same removal of selenite by coprecipitation and by adsorption and concluded that a heterogeneous ion-exchange reaction takes place with the selenite ion and freshly precipitated metal hydroxide.

Re-examining Figure 1 we see that in part of the field of selenite stability Fe^{3+} is reduced to Fe^{2+} which might liberate the selenite ion in a soluble form. In a reducing environment below the dashed line in Figure 1, a large region of Fe^{2+} exists and here SeO_3^{2-} Se^0 or Se^{2-} might be found, depending on whether equilibrium

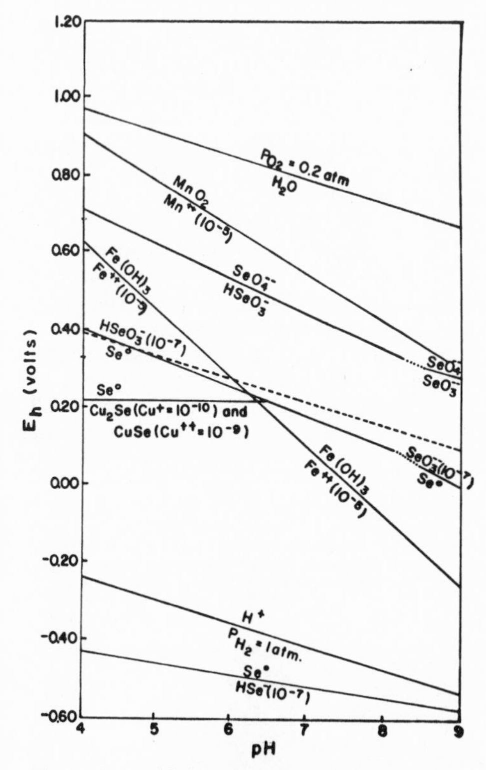

Figure 1. Oxidation-reduction potentials of selenium couples and other redox couples versus pH (*from* Geering and others, 1968).

conditions are realized. In this region of Eh-pH conditions sedimentary pyrite (FeS_2) is formed and is frequently enriched in selenium that substitutes for the sulfur.

In the Eh-pH region above the SeO_3^{2-}/SeO_4^{2-} line we find that dissolved oxygen offers the highest potential for oxidizing selenite to selenate and that the difference in potential between the O^2/H_2O couples and SeO_4^{2-}/SeO_3^{2-} increases with increasing pH. Thus, we would expect the selenate ion to be favored in an alkaline environment and this is where it has been found—in alkaline soils in semiarid regions. If it were formed in soils of humid regions one would expect the soils to be depleted of selenium. In fact, Hawaiian soils beneath 100 in. of rainfall per year contain as much as 15 ppm selenium in the surface horizon, indicating ferric-oxide-bound selenite ions.

Carter and others (1969) added $BaSeO_4$ and $CuSeO_4$ separately to plots with a 1-yr-old stand of alfalfa growing in an alkaline silt loam near Kimberly, Idaho (Table 3). They found that 1 kg per hectare of selenium in either form produced toxic alfalfa; the $CuSeO_4$ is much more available than the barium salt.

ORGANIC CHEMISTRY OF SELENIUM IN SOILS

Microorganisms play a role in the chemistry of selenium in soils that has not been measured, but is certainly important in the selenium cycle. The water-soluble selenium in South Dakota soils usually increases with depth in the soil profile (Olson and others, 1942). An illustration of this distribution is given in Table 4 taken from the work of Abu-Erreish and others (1968), who studied the evolution of volatile selenium from the soil. To test the volatility of selenium in these soils, 90 g of soil (M-94)

TABLE 3. SELENIUM CONTENT OF ALFALFA RESULTING FROM APPLICATIONS OF BARIUM SELENATE AND CUPRIC SELENATE TO PORTNEUF SILT LOAM, NEAR KIMBERLY, IDAHO (Carter and others, 1969)

Selenium application (Kg/ha)	Form applied	Selenium content (ppm) in dry alfalfa*	
		2d cutting (1966)	2d cutting (1967)
0.0	..	0.12	0.13
0.5	$BaSeO_4$	0.98	1.58
1.0	do.	4.26	2.69
2.0	do.	6.05	5.87
4.0	do.	12.68	13.27
1.0	$CuSeO_4$	27.85	3.20

* Values are means of three replications.

TABLE 4. TOTAL AND WATER-SOLUBLE SELENIUM IN SOUTH DAKOTA SOIL PROFILE (Abu-Erreish and others, 1968, Table 1)

Sample no.	Texture and depth (inches)	pH	Total selenium (ppm)	Water-soluble selenium (ppm)
M-92	Clay, 0-12	7.7	6.6	0.083
M-93	Clay, 12-24	..	6.9	1.0
M-94	Clay, 24-36	7.9	9.1	2.6

were mixed with 10 g of vermiculite and 5 g of wheat. Air was bubbled through water, then through the moist soil mixture, and finally through nitric acid to collect any evolved selenium. Mold growth increased with time and with moisture content of the soil up to 24.4 percent water and decreased at 28.3 percent water. The selenium that was evolved also increased with time and with moisture content of the soil up to 24.4 percent water and decreased at 28.3 percent water. These authors also found that the evolution of selenium was reduced 80 to 85 percent by autoclaving the soil prior to the experiment—suggesting that the active organism that releases selenium in a volatile form was derived primarily from the soil. Radioactive Se^{75} was evolved in similar experiments with the addition of $Na_2Se^{75}O_3$ to the soil.

Koval'skii and others (1968) isolated bacteria, actinomycetes, and molds from soils containing 0.5 ppm and 0.1 ppm selenium. Microorganisms from the high-selenium soils grew better at high-selenium concentrations in the medium than those from low-selenium soils. All of the microorganisms studied concentrated selenium inside their cells; the selenium content of the dry cells reached a concentration of 0.18 percent. Adaptation and resistance to high-selenium concentrations were proportional to the ability of organisms to reduce selenium to the elementary state.

Hidiroglou and others (1968) have demonstrated that rumen bacteria are capable of metabolizing inorganic selenium and incorporating the element into the microbic protein. Probably, similar organisms are present in soils.

Selenium is associated with the organic matter in soils as a residuum of seleniferous proteins in decaying plants and microorganisms, as elemental selenium in the remains of certain microorganisms and as reduced or bound selenites derived from water-soluble selenium. Rosenfield and Beath (1964), quoting work of Beath, reported that aqueous extracts of seleniferous species of *Astragalus* in a culture solution provide selenium to alfalfa in a form not injurious to the plant; 5 ppm Se as sodium selenite also in a culture solution yielded 15 g dry weight of alfalfa, whereas the same concentration of selenium in the *Astragalus* extract yielded 48.5 g dry weight of plant containing 441 ppm selenium.

TABLE 5. SELENIUM IN A TOXIC SOIL PROFILE, MEATH COUNTY, IRELAND (Fleming, 1962)

Depth (in.)	pH	Organic matter (percent)	Selenium (ppm)
0-6	6.5	28.7	360
6-12	6.5	44.5	1200
12-18	8.1	0.6	217

Highly seleniferous soils in Limerick, Tipperary, and Meath Counties of Ireland (Fleming, 1962) are characterized by high-organic matter (Table 5) and by toxic vegetation (Table 6). Fleming suggested that the selenium in these soils is, in part, complexed by organic matter.

SELENIUM IN PLANTS

The uptake of selenium by plants is governed first of all by the presence and availability of this element in the soils. When selenium is present and a fraction of a part per million is in an available form, plants vary in their uptake of selenium from species to species, with stage of growth, and season.

Certain species of *Astragalus* utilize selenium in an amino acid peculiar to these species: they absorb many times as much selenium as do other plants growing in the same soil. It has been suggested that they require selenium as a nutrient because of their unique selenium chemistry and because they have been found growing only in seleniferous soils (Shrift, 1969).

Several plants, usually those requiring much sulfur, absorb an intermediate amount of available selenium (among these are cabbage, mustard, and onions).

TABLE 6. SELENIUM CONTENT OF DIFFERENT PLANTS GROWN IN IRISH SELENIFEROUS SOILS (Fleming, 1962)

Plant	Selenium (ppm) in oven-dry matter
Wheat grain	39
White clover	153
Lettuce leaves	56
Cabbage leaves	409
Turnip roots	204
Cress leaves	212

Grasses and grain crops absorb low to moderate amounts of selenium. Wheat grain, however, is usually higher in selenium content than corn. Patrias and Olson (1969) found corn grown in the Midwestern States to be generally deficient in selenium as a total feed for farm animals generally and for chickens in particular. It is, perhaps, fortunate that the great wheat-producing areas of the world are in relatively dry areas where soils can have a maximum of available selenium. Thus, the grain consumed by wheat-eating peoples usually provides adequate selenium in the diet.

Where sufficient available selenium occurs in the soil, all species of plants will take up selenium in concentrations harmful to animals. The emphasis in recent years on the selenium accumulator species, such as certain *Astragalus* species, has tended to suggest undue importance for these plants in farm-animal poisoning. Farmers in parts of South Dakota had serious livestock troubles prior to the early 1930's. To illustrate, a farm known locally as the Reed farm changed owners repeatedly, usually with a lawsuit charging misrepresentation filed by the new owners against the previous owners. Families living on the Reed farm found that their horses and cattle sickened and became valueless; their chicken eggs failed to hatch and when the shells of the incubated eggs were broken, grossly deformed chicks were found that were incapable of breaking their way out of the egg. Kurt W. Franke of the South Dakota Agriculture Experiment Station found that these chick monstrosities occurred in eggs from hens fed wheat grain. He brought his problem to the U.S. Department of Agriculture where it was found that the wheat contained toxic amounts of selenium. Selenium compounds injected into the air sack of eggs also produced chick deformities resembling those caused by the toxic grain (Franke and others, 1936). Selenium poisoning was first identified in seleniferous wheat grain grown on certain farms in South Dakota. The seleniferous character of certain *Astragalus* species and other range plants was established independently by O. A. Beath, University of Wyoming.

By the middle of the 1930's the badly affected farms of South Dakota had been purchased by the Federal government and the "Reed farm" tragedies ended. The Reed farm is now a subagricultural experiment station of South Dakota. Fortunately soils that produce toxic crop plants are not widespread (Kubota and others, 1967), and even in their worst occurrences are variably seleniferous within a given acreage.

Seleniferous (harmful) vegetation has been reported in many areas of the world. Muth and Allaway (1963) report the occurrence of vegetation containing 50 ppm Se in 15 states of the United States. Three provinces of Canada have localities that have produced toxic seleniferous plants. Countries in which possibly toxic seleniferous vegetation occurs are listed in Table 7.

TABLE 7. COUNTRIES IN WHICH POSSIBLY TOXIC SELENIFEROUS VEGETATION HAS BEEN REPORTED

Country	Reference
United States	Muth and Allaway (1963)
Canada	Byers and Lakin (1939)
Mexico	Byers (1937)
England and Wales	Webb and others (1966)
Ireland	Walsh and Fleming (1952)
Israel	Ravikovitch & Margolin (1957a)
Colombia	Ancizar-Sordo (1947)
Argentina	De Salas (1947)
Venezuela	Jaffe and others (1969)
Central African Republic	do.
Madagascar	do.
Nigeria	do.
Kenya	do.
Japan	do.
India	Zalkind and Ermakov (1968)
Republic of South Africa	Brown and de Wet (1962)
Australia	do.

SELENIUM POISONING OF ANIMALS

Different forms of selenium poisoning of livestock have been reported. The effects on animal health due to excessive selenium differ with the chemical form of the selenium compounds in the animal diet. Maag and Glenn (1967) stated that cattle fed inorganic selenium salts developed few signs of typical alkali disease or blind staggers. They observed striking differences in the effects by feeding inorganic selenium and by feeding seleniferous plants to animals. The brief descriptions of various types of selenium poisoning that follow are those occurring in seleniferous areas. The selenium in the diet of these animals is probably organically bound in plant food stuff with small amounts of additional inorganic selenium in drinking water.

Acute poisoning of cattle and sheep occurs when herds or bands are being driven from one pasturage to another. Animals, under these conditions, eat forage indiscriminately and many may die overnight. Both seleniferous *Astragalus* species and alkaloids are probably involved. Such losses have been reported in Wyoming and Colorado.

Subacute poisoning, known locally as blind staggers, loco disease, or pushing disease, has been reported in western United States (Rosenfeld and Beath, 1964) and in South Africa (Brown and de Wet, 1962). This is probably another instance of the confusion between selenium toxicity and naturally toxic vegetation. The actual cause of these diseases is in debate (James and others, 1967).

Chronic poisoning is caused by daily ingestion of cereals and grasses containing 5 to 20 ppm selenium. Animals suffering from chronic selenium poisoning are stiff and lame; they lose weight and fail to respond to good care. Loss of hair and abnormal growth of hoofs are prominent symptoms. The liver, kidneys, and heart show scarred tissues in postmortem examinations. This typical selenium poisoning has been reported in western United States, Mexico, Ireland, and Israel. Chronic human poisoning of this type has been reported in Mexico (Byers, 1937) and Colombia (Ancizar-Sordo, 1947).

Subchronic poisoning has been reported by Brown and de Wet (1962) in South Africa. They report livers of animals containing as much as 30 ppm selenium on a wet weight basis and suggest that the moderate selenium content of the diets of these animals has weakened them and made them more susceptible to disease.

In summary, acute and subacute selenium poisoning is compounded with naturally toxic range-plant poisoning and is difficult to evaluate. Chronic selenium poisoning is more clearly demonstrated and occurs in many areas of the world. Fortunately, the human diet is rarely restricted solely to the products of a highly seleniferous area. Thus, selenium poisoning through the food-plant cycle is rare in the world human population and tends to be restricted to combinations of highly seleniferous areas whose populations depend largely on local agricultural produce.

TABLE 8. SELENIUM CONTENT OF VARIOUS SAMPLES OF PAPER, COAL, AND PETROLEUM

Material	Selenium (ppm) Average	Maximum	Reference
Newspaper	8.6	18.3	Johnson (1970)
Cardboard	2.8	5.1	do.
Laboratory tissue	7.1	19.5	do.
Cigarette paper	0.17		Nadkarni & Ehmann (1969)
Raw petroleum	0.92	0.95	Hashimoto & others (1970)
Heavy petroleum fractions	0.99	1.65	do.
Coal (Tokyo market)	1.18	1.30	do.
U.S. crude petroleum	0.17	0.35	Pillay and others (1969)
U.S. coal	3.2	10.65	do.

DISPERSION OF SELENIUM IN OUR ENVIRONMENT

Selenium in minute concentrations, but appreciable quantities, is being released in our environment daily by burning petroleum products, solid wastes, and coal (Hashimoto and others, 1970).

Johnson (1970) found 1.6 to 19 ppm Se in newspaper, cardboard, and laboratory tissue (Table 8). He estimates that paper is 70 percent of the billion pounds of solid waste collected per day in the United States. He found as much as 14.5 ppm Se in the particulate matter collected in an incinerator stack emission sample.

Hashimoto and others (1970) reported about 1 ppm Se in petroleum and coal used in Tokyo, Japan, and vicinity. They also reported that the rubber in automobile tires used in the Tokyo area contained 0.7 to 2.0 ppm Se. Soils there contained 1.0 to 1.3 ppm Se and soil extracts 0.5 ppm. The high value (0.5 ppm Se) of the soil extracts suggests that selenium contamination may be approaching toxic levels near that large industrial city.

In contrast to the relatively uniform selenium content of petroleum and coal found in Tokyo by Hashimoto and his associates, Pillay and others (1969) found selenium to average only 0.17 ppm in 39 samples of U.S. crude oil samples, and range from 0.06 to 0.35 ppm. Pillay and his associates, however, found much selenium in U.S. coal samples—86 samples

TABLE 9. SELENIUM CONTENT OF FISH MEAL (Kifer and others, 1969)

Fish sampled	Selenium (ppm) Average	Range
East Canadian herring	1.95	1.3-2.6
Chilean anchovetta	1.35	0.84-2.6
Tuna	4.63	3.4-6.2
Smelt	0.95	0.49-1.23
Menhaden	2.09	0.75-4.2

averaged 3.2 ppm Se and ranged from 0.46 to 10.65 ppm. Eleven samples of coal from Pennsylvania ranged from 1.35 to 10.65 ppm and averaged 3.74 ppm Se. It is, perhaps, significant that the highest selenium content of twelve rivers of the world was found in the Susquehanna River, which drains coal mining areas of Pennsylvania (Kharkar and others, 1968).

Nadkarni and Ehmann (1969) found from 0.21 to 1.31 ppm Se in cigarette tobacco and 0.17 ppm in cigarette paper. Johnson (1970) reported 2.8 to 8.6 ppm as the average selenium content of various types of paper (Table 8).

The escape of SeO_2 and to a lesser extent of Se^0 during the melting of selenium-containing steel has been reported by Ershov (1969). Selenium-containing stainless steels are a very small output of the steel industry. Selenium in the atmosphere in the immediate neighborhood of electrolytic copper-refining plants is reported to be 0.5 $\mu g/m^3$ and only 0.07 $\mu g/m^3$ at a distance of 2 km (Selyankina and Alekseeva, 1970).

Selenium is present in phosphate rocks (Robbins and Carter, 1970) and in superphosphate produced from them. Superphosphate containing 20 ppm or more selenium may provide sufficient selenium to the plants in selenium-deficient areas to protect livestock from selenium-deficiency diseases, according to Robbins and Carter.

Table 9 shows the marked variation in the selenium content of fish meals both within and between species. The tuna is particularly high in selenium (Kifer and others, 1969). This concentration of selenium by fish from waters extremely low in selenium suggests that selenium contamination of streams or lakes may, like mercury, yield dangerously high selenium content in fish taken for human consumption.

SUMMARY

Soils producing crop plants that are toxic because of selenium are confined to small areas but occur throughout the world. Such soils are confined to semiarid regions or areas of impeded drainage. They contribute no significant hazard to human health and only locally to animal health.

Environmental contamination with selenium is increasing but will probably stay well below a hazardous concentration. Locally, mining and industrial wastes may produce minor hazards. However, the effect of added selenium in the atmosphere and waters in combination with other contaminants is not known and should be studied.

REFERENCES CITED

Abu-Erreish, G. M., Whitehead, E. I., and Olson, O. E., 1968, Evolution of volatile selenium from soils: Soil Sci., 106, no. 6, p. 415–420.

Ancizar-Sordo, Jorge, 1947, Occurrence of selenium in soils and plants of Colombia, South America: Soil Sci., v. 63, no. 6, p. 437–438.

Brown, J.M.M., and de Wet, P. J., 1962, A preliminary report on the occurrence of selenosis in South Africa and its possible role in the aetiology of tribulosis (Geeldikkop), enzootic icterus and some other disease conditions encountered in the Karoo areas: Onderstepoort Jour. Veterinary Research, v. 29, no. 1, p. 111–135.

Byers, H. G., 1937, Selenium in Mexico: Indus. and Eng. Chemistry, v. 29, no. 10, p. 1200–1202.

Byers, H. G., and Lakin, H. W., 1939, Selenium in Canada: Canadian Jour. Research, v. 17, p. 364–369.

Byers, H. G., Miller, J. T., Williams, K. T., and Lakin, H. W., 1938, Selenium occurrence in certain soils in the United States with a discussion of related topics—III: U.S. Dept. Agriculture Tech. Bull. 601, 74 p.

Carter, D L., Brown, M. J., and Robbins, C. W., 1969, Selenium concentrations in alfalfa from several sources applied to a low selenium, alkaline soil: Soil Sci. Soc. America Proc., v. 33, no. 5, p. 715–718.

De Salas, S. M., 1947, Contenido enselenio de algunas aguas Argentinas, 3ª parte *of* El selenio en las aguas: Argentina Adm. Nac. Agua Rev., v. 11, p. 21–24.

Ershov, V. P., 1969, Hygienic characteristics of the selenium-containing steel production and prevention of selenium poisoning [in Russian]: Gigiena Truda Prof. Zabolevaniya, v. 13, no. 12, p. 29–33.

Fleming, G. A., 1962, Selenium in Irish soils and plants: Soil Sci., v. 94, no. 1, p. 28–35.

Fleming, G. A., and Walsh, T., 1957, Selenium occurrence in certain Irish soils and its toxic effects on animals: Royal Irish Acad. Proc., v. 58, Sec. b, no. 7, p. 151–165.

Franke, K. W., Moxon, A. L., Poley, W. E., and Tully, W. C., 1936, Monstrosities produced by the injection of selenium salts into hens' eggs: Anatom. Rec., v. 65, no. 1, p. 15–22.

Ganapathy, R., Keays, R. R., and Anders, Edward, 1970, Apollo 12 lunar samples—Trace element analysis of a core and the uniformity of the regolith: Science, v. 170, no. 3957, p. 533–535.

Geering, H. R., Cary, E. E., Jones, L.H.P., and Allaway, W. H., 1968, Solubility and redox criteria for the possible forms of selenium in soils: Soil Sci. Soc. America Proc., v. 32, no. 1, p. 35–40.

Goldschmidt, V. M., 1954, Geochemistry [Alex Muir, ed.]: Oxford Univ. Press, 730 p.

Gregers-Hansen, Birte, 1967, Application of radioactivation analysis for the determination of selenium and cobalt in soils and plants: Internat. Cong. Soil Sci., 8th, Bucharest, 1964, Trans., v. 3, p. 63–70.

Hashimoto, Yoshikazu, Hwang, J. Y., and Yanagisawa, Saburo, 1970, Possible source of atmospheric pollution of selenium: Environmental Sci. and Technology, v. 4, no. 2, p. 157–158.

Hidiroglou, M., Heaney, D. P., and Jenkins, K. J., 1968, Metabolism of inorganic selenium in rumen bacteria: Canadian Jour. Physiology and Pharmacology, v. 46, no. 2, p. 229–232.

Jaffe, W. G., Chavez, J. F., and Mondragon, M. C., 1969, Selenium content of sesame samples from different countries [in Spanish]: Archivos Latinoamericanos Nutricion, v. 19, no. 3, p. 299–307.

James, L. F., Shupe, J. L., Binns, Wayne, and Keeler, R. F., 1967, Abortive and teratogenic effects of locoweed on sheep and cattle: Am. Jour. Veterinary Research, v. 28, no. 126, p. 1379–1388.

Johnson, Henry, 1970, Determination of selenium in solid waste: Environmental Sci. and Technology, v. 4, no. 10, p. 850–853.

Kharkar, D. P., Turekian, K. K., and Bertine, K. K., 1968, Stream supply of dissolved silver, molybdenum, antimony, selenium, chromium, cobalt, rubidium and cesium to the oceans: Geochim. et Cosmochim. Acta, v. 32, no. 3, p. 285–298.

Kifer, R. R., Payne, W. L., and Ambrose, M. E., 1969, Selenium content of fish meals—II: Feedstuffs, v. 41, no. 51, p. 24–25.

Koval'skii, V. V., Ermakov, V. V., and Letunova, S. V., 1968, Geochemical ecology of microorganisms under conditions of different selenium content in soils [in Russian]: Mikrobiologiya, v. 37, no. 1, p. 122–130.

Kubota, J., Allaway, W. H., Carter, D. L., Gary, E. E., and Lazar, V. A., 1967, Selenium in crops in the United States in relation to selenium-responsive diseases of animals: Jour. Agriculture and Food Chemistry, v. 15, no. 3, p. 448–453.

Maag, D. D., and Glenn, M. W., 1967, Toxicity of selenium: Farm animals, *in* Muth, O. H., Oldfield, J. E., and Weswig, P. H., eds., Selenium in biomedicine, 1st Internat. Symp., Oregon State University, 1966, Westport, Conn., The AVI Publ. Co., Inc., p. 127–140.

Muth, O. H., and Allaway, W. H., 1963, The relationship of white muscle disease to the distribution of naturally occurring selenium: Am. Veterinary Med. Assoc. Jour., v. 142, no. 12, p. 1379–1384.

Nadkarni, R. A., and Ehmann, W. D., 1969, Determination of trace elements in the reference cigarette tobacco by neutron activation analysis: Radiochem. and Radioanal. Letters, v. 2, no. 3, p. 161–168.

Olson, O. E., Whitehead, E. I., and Moxon, A. L., 1942, Occurrence of soluble selenium in soils and its availability to plants: Soil Sci., v. 54, p. 47–53.

Patrias, George, and Olson, O. E., 1969, Selenium contents of samples of corn from Midwestern States: Feedstuffs, v. 41, no. 43, p. 32, 34.

Pillay, K.K.S., Thomas, C. C., Jr., and Kaminski, J. W., 1969, Neutron activation analysis of the selenium content of fossil fuels: Nuclear Applications and Technology, v. 7, no. 5, p. 478–483.

Plotnikov, V. I., and Kochetkov, V. L., 1967, The effect of metal hydroxides on the sorption of selenite ions [in Russian]: Akad. Nauk. Kazakh, SSR Izv. Ser. Fiz.-Mat., v. 5, no. 2, p. 66–70.

Rankama, Kalervo, and Sahama, Th. G., 1950, Geochemistry: Chicago, Chicago Univ. Press, 912 p.

Ravikovitch, S., and Margolin, M., 1957a, Selenium in soils and plants: Rehovot, Agricultural Research Sta., 1957 Ser. no. 145-E, v. 7, no. 2–3, p. 41–52.

—— 1957b, Hindering effects of barium chloride and calcium sulfate on selenium absorption by alfalfa: Israel Sci. Soc. Convention Proc. 2, Biology and Geology Bull. 6B, p. 265.

Robbins, C. W., and Carter, D. L., 1970, Selenium concentrations in phosphorus fertilizer materials and associated uptake by plants: Soil Sci. Soc. America Proc., v. 34, no. 3, p. 506–509.

Roberts, R. C., and party, 1942, Soil survey of Puerto Rico: U.S. Dept. Agriculture Soil Survey Ser. 1936, no. 8, 503 p.

Rosenfeld, Irene, and Beath, O. A., 1964, Selenium; geobotany, biochemistry, toxicity, and nutrition: Academic Press, 411 p.

Schwarz, Klaus, and Foltz, C. M., 1957, Selenium as an integral part of factor 3 against dietary necrotic liver degeneration: Am. Chem. Soc. Jour., v. 79, p. 3292–3293.

Selyankina, K. P., and Alekseeva, L. S., 1970, Selenium and tellurium in the atmosphere in the vicinity of copper electrolytic refining plants [in Russian]: Gigiena Sanitariya, v. 35, no. 3, p. 95–96.

Shrift, Alex, 1969, Aspects of selenium metabolism in higher plants: Ann. Rev. Plant Physiology, v. 20, p. 475–494.

Swaine, D. J., 1955, The trace-element content of soils: Harpenden, England, Commonwealth Bur. Soil Sci. Tech. Commun. 48, 157 p.

Turekian, K. K., and Wedepohl, K. H., 1961, Distribution of the elements in some major units of the earth's crust: Geol. Soc. America Bull., v. 72, no. 2, p. 175–191.

Vinogradov, A. P., 1959, The geochemistry of rare and dispersed chemical elements in soils [2d

ed.]: New York, Consultants Bur., 209 p.
Walsh, T., and Fleming, G. A., 1952, Selenium levels in rocks, soils, and herbage from a high selenium locality in Ireland: Internat. Soc. Soil Sci., Comm. II and IV, Trans., v. 2, p. 178–183.
Webb, J. S., Thornton, I., and Fletcher, K., 1966, Seleniferous soils in parts of England and Wales: Nature, v. 211, no. 5046, p. 327.
Williams, K. T., and Byers, H. G., 1936, Selenium compounds in soils: Indus. and Eng. Chemistry, v. 28, no 8, p. 912–914
Zalkind, F. L., and Ermakov, V. V., 1968, Selenium content of the seeds of grain crops and lathyrism [in Russian]: Agrokhimiya, no. 6, p. 98–107.

Manuscript Received by the Society June 10, 1971
Publication Authorized by the Director, U.S. Geological Survey
Published in The Geological Society of America Bulletin, January, 1972.

The Geological Society of America, Inc.
Special Paper 140, 1972

Selenium Accumulation in Soils: Discussion and Reply

DISCUSSION

D. V. Frost
48 High Street, Brattleboro, Vermont 05301

One of Dr. Lakin's slides showed selenium values for various solid wastes as reported from a government laboratory (Johnson, 1970). An average for newspaper is reported as more than 8 ppm Se. West (1967) had reported 6 to 10 ppm of Se in cigarette and cigar papers and had suggested selenium as a possible cause of lung cancer and emphysema from smoking.

To help settle the question, I purchased and analyzed cigarette paper and sent samples to Oscar Olson, W. H. Allaway, and John L. Martin. None of us found appreciable levels of Se in any samples of paper. Cardboard made with glue contained more Se than newspaper, apparently in the glue, but none contained as much as 0.1 ppm Se. After much difficulty Olson managed to get these results published (Olson and Frost, 1969). Two months later Henry Johnson's disparate values (1970) for Se in newspaper and tissue appeared. Noting the alleged carcinogenicity of Se as part of the problem, Johnson cited West and Cimmerman (1964, 1967), but failed to note that there is no published evidence clearly establishing such a cause-effect relationship. The Toxicology Division of the Food and Drug Administration has indicated that the original work actually failed to produce unequivocal evidence for carcinogenicity of Se (Fitzhugh and Friedman, 1970, written commun.).

Careful restudy of the question at Oregon State University, funded by the National Cancer Institute, showed no cancers attributable to any level of long-term selenite or selenate feeding (Harr and others, 1967). On the contrary, evidence has emerged indicating possible value of nutrient levels of Se, in instances where dietary Se may be marginal, to inhibit carcinogenesis (Shamberger, 1970; Shamberger and Frost, 1969). A number of studies are now underway to test this effect by way of controlled experiments in animals (Frost, 1970).

REFERENCES CITED

Frost, D. V., 1970, Tolerances for arsenic and selenium. A psychodynamic problem: World Rev. Pest Control, v. 9, p. 6–28.

Harr, J. R., Done, J. F., Tinsley, I. J., Weswig, P. H., and Yamamoto, R. S., 1967, Selenium toxicity in rats. II. Histopathology, *in* Muth, O. H., Symposium: Selenium in Biomedicine: Westport, Conn., AVI Publishing Co., p. 153–178.

Johnson, H., 1970, Determination of selenium in solid waste: Environmental Sci. and Technology, v.4, p. 850–853.

Olson, O. E., and Frost, D. V., 1970, Selenium in papers and tobacco: Environmental Sci. and Technology, v. 4, p. 686–687.

Shamberger, R. J., and Frost, D. V., 1969, Possible protective effect of selenium against human cancer: Canada Med. Assoc. Jour., v. 100, p. 682.

Shamberger, R. J., 1970, Relationship of selenium to cancer. I. Inhibitory effect of selenium on carcinogenesis: Natl. Cancer Inst. Jour., v. 44, p. 931–936.

West, P. W., 1967, Selenium-containing morganics in paper may play cancer role: Chem. and Eng. News, v. 45, p. 12–13.

Manuscript Received by the Society August 16, 1971
Published in The Geological Society of America Bulletin, January, 1972.

REPLY

Hubert W. Lakin
U.S. Geological Survey, Denver, Colorado 80225

It is difficult to reconcile data from reputable laboratories when the estimates of selenium content vary so greatly. Nadkarni and Ehmann (1969) give 0.17 ppm Se for cigarette papers that they analyzed. Elements not required by the plant are sometimes stored in the woody tissue: this could be an explanation for the presence of selenium in paper prepared from wood and could also explain a great variability in selenium content. Additional careful work must be done to resolve these large differences in selenium content of paper.

REFERENCES CITED

Nadkarni, R. A., and Ehmann, W. D., 1969, Determination of trace elements in the reference cigarette tobacco by neutron activation analysis: Radiochemistry and Radioanalytic Letters, v. 2, p. 161–168.

Manuscript Received by the Society August 16, 1971

Published in The Geological Society of America Bulletin, January, 1972.

PRINTED IN U.S.A.

The Geological Society of America, Inc.
Special Paper 140, 1972

Selenium Deficiency in Soils and Its Effect on Animal Health

J. E. Oldfield
Department of Animal Science, Oregon State University, Corvallis, Oregon 97331

ABSTRACT

Selenium in minute quantities has been shown to be a dietary essential for animal life, and soil-plant-animal relations have been identified in the distribution of the element. In some cases, soils are frankly deficient in selenium—most particularly those derived from igneous rocks, and the deficiency in surface layers may be aggravated by intensive irrigation. Alternatively, soil selenium may exist in a form that is either unavailable to plants or absorbed by them with difficulty. Representative of such a form is the highly insoluble ferric oxide-selenite complex which frequently occurs in high-moisture, acid soils. Uptake of selenium by plants may also be inhibited by presence of interfering substances in the soil, such as sulphur, or it may be enhanced by liming. Analytical surveys have revealed also that considerable variation exists among plant species in their abilities to take up and retain selenium from the soil. Legumes have been consistently implicated as forages conducive to white muscle disease, a selenium-responsive myopathy, and New Zealand observations have shown white clover (*Trifolium repens* L.) to contain significantly lower levels of selenium than grasses, and particularly a native grass, browntop (*Agrostis tenuis* Sibth.). In addition to the differences in absolute selenium uptake, it has been suggested that some plants, and again legumes are suspect, may contain organic inhibitors of selenium utilization by livestock. Some experiments have investigated the effectiveness of additions of selenium to the soil in overcoming selenium deficiency among farm animals. Protection for 2 yrs has been achieved by this technique; however, the various factors influencing the soil-plant-animal relations of selenium direct caution in its application.

INTRODUCTION

In 1965, Douglas Frost engagingly documented the changes that have recently taken place in the understanding of selenium's effects upon animal life: "Just when the detectives had caught up with selenium in all its rascality—impugned as a carcinogen, and about the only element sly enough to be taken up by plants at high enough levels to poison animals—selenium played its trump card. It became an essential nutrient," (Frost, 1965). The knowledge of selenium's essential status was accumulated stepwise. First, Schwarz and Foltz (1957) demonstrated that selenium would protect rats fed Torula yeast diets from necrotic liver degeneration, following which it was found similarly protective against exudative diathesis in poultry (Patterson and others, 1957) and against white muscle disease (WMD) in young ruminants (Muth and others, 1958). These isolated instances led to the recognition of several selenium-responsive diseases, which affected a number of different animal species in widely separated parts of the world (Sharman, 1960). Finally, by the use of carefully controlled experimental diets, uncomplicated selenium deficiency was produced in Japanese quail (Thompson and Scott, 1968) and in rats (McCoy and Weswig, 1969).

In the course of these investigations, and particularly those relating to field cases of selenium-responsive disease, it became evident that a chain of relationships existed through the soil-plant-animal cycle involving selenium. Coupled with earlier knowledge of selenium toxicity (Trelease and Beath, 1949), it appeared that these relationships might operate across a very broad spectrum of selenium levels. Presence of high levels of selenium in certain soils had been known for some time and were catalogued by Lakin, (1961). The identification of such seleniferous soils was aided by the discovery (Beath and others, 1934) that certain indicator plants, which had the ability to accumulate high levels of the element, grew in high-selenium areas. These plants were shown to be involved in selenosis of animals (Beath and others, 1932). The other end of the scale, now recognized as selenium deficiency, has been less completely charted. In a large part this has been due to the analytical difficulties involved in coping with what Schwarz (1961) has called the "elusive qualities of the element," although some significant advances have occurred in this country (Kubota and others, 1967). The soil-plant-animal relations in selenium deficiency are less clear, and have caused Allaway (1968a) to remark, "In few, if any, of these (deficiency) cases was the occurrence of the problem predicted in advance on the basis of the geology of these areas." On the other hand, reasonably direct relationships have been described between levels of selenium in plants and incidence of selenium deficiency (WMD) in animals (Allaway and Hodgson, 1964). Thus, involvement of interfering factors in the transmission of low levels of selenium from the soil, through plants to animals was implied, and these factors form the basis for much of this paper.

SIGNS OF SELENIUM DEFICIENCY

There are two major signs of selenium deficiency in animals: liver necrosis, which has been repeatedly demonstrated under controlled experimental conditions in rats and mice, and a similar condition, called hepatosis dietetica, in swine, and a myopathy which frequently occurs under field conditions in young ruminants and in poultry. The muscle damage may be accompanied by calcification, as in WMD of calves and lambs or by exudation of cellular fluids into extracellular space, as in exudative diathesis of poultry. Frequently associated with such specific signs of selenium deficiency are poor growth of hair or feathers, and general depression of rate of body growth. These relationships suggest the association of selenium with the protein moieties of the tissues of animals, and such has proven to be the case (Ganther, 1965). The frequency of occurrence of WMD in cattle and sheep in certain areas provides at least circumstantial evidence for a soil-plant-animal relationship, since these animals, probably more than most others, are restricted in their diets to locally grown forages.

SELENIUM-DEFICIENT SOILS

It seems possible that some, at least, of the cases of selenium deficiency in livestock owe their origin to an uncomplicated deficiency of the element in the soils on which feeds for the animals were grown. Anyone who has suffered through the difficulties of retaining minute amounts of selenium through destructive analytical procedures is well aware of the element's volatility in the presence of heat. Several investigators have noted the escape of large quantities of sulphur, and lesser quantities of selenium, from volcanic systems in the form of volatile gases (*see* Lakin and Davidson, 1967). These authors state, ". . . the soils derived from igneous rocks are most likely to be uniformly deficient in selenium." It is noteworthy that much of the soil in the eastern parts of Washington and Oregon and in northern California, which is described as the source of "very low" selenium levels in crops (Kubota and others, 1967; Carter and others, 1968) is of fairly recent, volcanic origin. Much of this area is presently subject to fairly strong prevailing winds from the Pacific coast, which, if they occurred historically, might have dispersed the selenium volatilized in the deposition of soil parent material to the eastward. The residual volcanic soil roughly coincides with areas where WMD is a fairly frequent and serious occurrence (Muth and Allaway, 1963).

The deficiency of soil selenium may be aggravated by irrigation, and again, it is pertinent that one of the areas of most severe incidence of WMD, near Madras, Oregon, has been subjected to intensive irrigation in recent years. Although specific data from this area are not available, there have been studies made elsewhere on the effects of leaching upon soil selenium. Williams and Byers (1935) showed in studies of the alkaline, seleniferous soils of the Gunnison and Colorado river basins that, while salts forming on the walls of drainage ditches in Mesa and Montrose Counties, Colorado, contained from 16 to 260 ppm selenium, the soils irrigated by the ditches rarely contained over 2 ppm. Fleming and Walsh (1957) also demonstrated effects of soil leaching upon selenium content by showing that Irish soils high on valley walls contained minimal levels of selenium (0.5 to 1.2 ppm); lower down they contained more (4.1 to 6.2 ppm) and on the poorly drained valley floor they contained surprising accumulations (63.4 to 225 ppm). Ravikovitch and Margolin (1957) provided further evidence of depletion of topsoil of selenium by continuous cropping when they demonstrated that alfalfa planted on virgin soil in Israel contained up to 44 ppm of selenium in the first crop year, but barely detectable amounts 3 yrs later. Investigations in Western Australia also implicated leaching losses in the low-selenium soil picture, in demonstrating an inverse relationship between soil selenium content and mean annual rainfall, although complications due to soil differences and length of time the land had been cropped were recognized (Gardiner and Gorman, 1963).

It seems reasonable to assume that, in addition to soils that are frankly deficient in selenium due to losses of the element either in the processes of their formation, or subsequently, others may exist in which selenium is present, but in a form unavailable to plant life. Elemental selenium, for example, can be found in soils treated with Na_2SeO_3. This form is not readily available to plants; nor surprisingly, is it easily oxidized to forms that are available. The extent to which elemental selenium is a naturally occurring soil constituent, however, is not well known. Where soil parent material weathers under humid conditions to form acid soils, its content of selenium is inclined to form highly insoluble ferric oxide-selenite complexes, which are also unusable by plants. Plants which contain insufficient selenium to meet the nutritional requirements of animals characteristically grow on acid soils formed from low-selenium rocks (Allaway, 1968a).

INTERFERING FACTORS IN SOILS

Quite early in the investigation of WMD in Oregon, it was observed that incidence of the disease was sometimes increased following the application of gypsum, $CaSO_4 \cdot 2H_2O$, to the soils on which forage for the animals' feed was grown (Muth, 1955). Antagonism between selenium and sulphur has been known for many years, and has been interpreted by Leggett and Epstein (1956), on the basis of results from studies of the kinetics of sulphate absorption by barley roots, as a competition between the two ions for an absorption site.

Davies and Watkinson (1966) compared the content of selenium in plants fertilized with sodium selenite alone, or mixed with superphosphate on a peat soil base, and found it lower where the superphosphate was included (0.57 *versus* 0.43 ppm, respectively). They attributed the lower content to preferential stimulation of the plant growth by the superphosphate-sulphur, rather than to competitive absorption between sulphate and selenite by the plants. There have been other indications, though, where sulphur-selenium competition does seem to have been directly involved. The uptake of selenium by winter wheat was decreased from 110 ppm to 2 ppm by application of gypsum or of elemental sulphur (Hurd-Karrer, 1935; Hurd-Karrer and Kennedy, 1936). Shrift (1961) reporting on studies conducted with *Chlorella vulgaris* suggested that at any one exogenous level of a selenium compound the concentration of cellular selenium falls with an increase of exogenous sulphur. Sulphate interference with selenium appears to operate at the soil-plant level rather than at the plant-animal level in the food chain, since, in Oregon studies, the supplementation of WMD-causative diets with sulphate did not increase the over-all incidence of the disease (Whanger and others, 1969). It has been suggested, however, that the very limited absorption of sulphate from the intestinal tract of animals may be an important deterrent to effective competition between sulphate and selenium in the animal (Ganther and Baumann, 1962).

Some circumstantial evidence has been provided that other inorganic elements may inhibit the uptake of selenium, from soil, by plants. Cannon (1969), for example, has reviewed the close relations that exist among uranium, molybdenum, selenium, and vanadium in certain soils. Taboury and Coudray-Viau (1939) presented data indicating that the concentrations of iron, manganese, magnesium, and lithium were higher in normal plants than in seleniferous plants. Of these, the relationship between iron and selenium has received more critical attention than the others. Allaway (1968b) has summarized this situation succinctly: "Selenites are very strongly bound by hydrous oxides of iron, and these iron oxide-selenite compounds or complexes are very insoluble from about *p*H 4 to *p*H 8.5."

Just as presence of certain ions in the soil inhibits the uptake of selenium by plants, the presence or effects of others may enhance it. The association of low-selenium forage with acid soils, previously mentioned, suggests a possible beneficial effect from liming certain selenium-deficient soils. The studies of Cary and others (1967) confirm that liming certain selenium-deficient soils will slightly increase the uptake of selenium by plants, but it is doubtful that this increased plant-selenium concentration would be significant in animal nutrition.

VARIATIONS IN UPTAKE OF SOIL-SELENIUM BY PLANTS

The soil-plant-animal cycle for selenium is further complicated by variations in the abilities of different plants to remove selenium from the soil and incorporate it in their tissues. The most dramatic variants are the selenium-accumulating plants, and Moxon and others (1950) have reported that *Stanleya pinnata* concentrated 2,380 ppm of selenium as compared with only 6.8 ppm in *Artemesia canadensis* grown in close proximity (an area of about 4 sq rods) on the same geological formation. There is some evidence that variation may also occur at the other end of the scale, and that certain forage plants may be more conducive to selenium-responsive diseases of animals than others, when grown on soils of low-selenium content or availability.

It has been observed in Oregon that field cases of WMD occur more frequently when legumes have been fed than grasses (Muth, 1963), and alfalfa has been commonly chosen as the basis for low-selenium experimental diets. This situation may reflect the choice of alfalfa as a means of improving irrigated rangeland, however, rather than inefficiency of selenium uptake by alfalfa. Beeson (1961) noted that little evidence existed which would suggest that alfalfa could absorb large quantities of selenium; however, extensive data assembled by Hamilton and Beath (1963) did not show alfalfa to be less efficient than many other plants, including range grasses and forbs, in removing selenium from soils containing measured amounts of either inorganic or organic selenium compounds. Roughan (1965) has observed that there is little evidence to suggest that, under natural conditions, legumes will take up less selenium from the soil than grasses. Alfalfa generally produces more forage than grasses, and its selenium content may be diluted by this greater amount of plant material.

In New Zealand, the central pumice plateau of the North Island is the site of extensive WMD and "ill-thrift" among lambs, both of which respond to administration of selenium. In this setting, Davies and Watkinson (1966) studied comparative efficiencies of selenium uptake by several indigenous species of pasture plants. Marked differences occurred between plant species in selenium uptake. Among the species studied, browntop (*Agrostis tenuis* Sibth.) consistently showed the highest concentration and white clover (*Trifolium repens* L.) the lowest concentration, with orchard grass (*Dactylis glomerata* L.) and perennial ryegrass (*Lolium perenne* L.) intermediate. The 3 grasses average selenium uptakes two to four times greater than that of the white clover. It is noteworthy that the highest incidences of selenium-responsive diseases in New Zealand livestock are associated with improved pastures, particularly lush swards rich in clover (Cousins and Cairney, 1961), and seldom with unimproved "browntop country." In contrast, little difference in selenium-75 uptake by wheat, ryegrass, red clover, and white clover was recorded by Peterson and Butler (1962). However, their studies were conducted in highly purified nutrient solutions, rather than in soil media.

INTERFERING FACTORS IN ANIMALS

There has been some evidence for years now that certain stress factors, either physical or chemical in nature, may aggravate or precipitate selenium deficiency. Muth (1955) observed in Oregon that outbreaks of WMD were apt to occur or to increase in intensity when periods of warm sunshine interspersed the usually cold weather at calving and lambing time. Similarly, Gardiner (1962) reported from Western Australia that deaths or sudden lameness were especially frequent when sheep were driven and excited during some operation, such as shearing, dipping, drenching, or vaccinating. This situation was examined experimentally in this country by Young and Keeler (1962), who tied up one leg of lambs born to ewes fed a low-selenium diet and found that the lesions of WMD appeared in the opposite functional limb only. The metabolism of selenium appears to be affected to some extent by the metabolism of vitamin E, and at least in some cases, WMD has occurred with concurrent selenium and vitamin E deficiencies. Blaxter's observations showed clearly that chemical stress could be imposed on animals that would cause myopathy by feeding pro-oxidants, such as highly unsaturated fish oils, which would destroy much of the dietary tocopherol (Blaxter and others, 1953).

Also, it would seem logical that, if selenium

supplies through the soil to forage plants are marginal, increased competition of animals for the limited selenium available might increase incidence of deficiencies. Gardiner (1969) has described such a situation in Western Australia, where stocking rates of sheep on pasture almost doubled over the decade 1957 through 1967. Similar intensification is taking place in this country, and in many other parts of the world. In addition to the competitive aspect already alluded to, this situation may be intensified by the cycling of selenium through sheep. In this process, microbial activity in the rumen has been shown to change organic forms of selenium, ingested in the plants to insoluble, inorganic forms returned to the soil in manure (Peterson and Spedding, 1963).

IMPROVEMENT OF FORAGE-SELENIUM LEVELS FROM LOW-SELENIUM SOILS

One of the strategies available for the prevention and control of WMD and other selenium-responsive diseases among foraging animals is the amendment of low-selenium soils with the deficient element. Grant (1965), in New Zealand, demonstrated the possibility of raising the selenium content of pasture forage in a selenium-deficient area by top-dressing the pasture with Na_2SeO_3 at rates up to 1 oz of actual selenium per acre. Selenate proved more efficient initially in raising forage selenium levels, but these elevated levels did not persist appreciably longer than those achieved with an equivalent amount of the cheaper, and more readily available, selenite. Elemental selenium was ineffective in increasing levels of forage selenium.

Grant's experiments were conducted on soils which were considered normal, or at worst only marginally deficient in selenium. Allaway and others (1966) studied the effects of selenium amendment of a frankly deficient soil near Madras, Oregon. A further point of difference was that the selenium, as Na_2SeO_3, was injected into the soil, in water solution, to a depth of about 10 cm, with a liquid fertilizer applicator. The rate of application was 1 ppm Se in the surface soil. Sufficient selenium was conveyed to alfalfa forage at this application rate to prevent WMD in lambs for up to 2 yrs postapplication. On the basis of five cuttings of alfalfa harvested, it was calculated that only 2 percent of the selenium applied to the soil had been removed with the crops. Unfortunately, further data on residual effects were unavailable.

Davies and Watkinson (1966) mixed sodium selenite with either monocalcium phosphate or superphosphate and applied it to pastures on a considerable range of soil types. They showed that the forage-selenium levels were higher following the monocalcium phosphate-mix than the superphosphate-mix, and that initial uptake of selenium was higher from peat soils than from mineral soils. This elevated uptake did not persist, however, and at about 300 days the selenium level in forage grown on peat had fallen below that considered adequate for animal health. Practical application of selenium to deficient soils is dependent upon the ability to avoid toxic levels in forage, as well as to achieve levels which are nutritionally adequate. Some encouragement on the former point has been provided by Ehlig and others (1968) who noted that differences in accumulation of selenium by "non-accumulator" forage plants grown on properly supplemented, low-selenium soils were small.

SUMMARY

This paper has attempted to document the soil-plant-animal cycle for selenium as it operates at "physiological" or "deficient" levels of the element. Pursuing the relationship in reverse order, there is a great, and growing, body of evidence of the existence of selenium-responsive diseases of livestock which occur all over the world. It seems probable, although by no means clear at this point, that the susceptibility of animals to such disease may be modified by factors other than selenium, notably vitamin E.

Consideration of the soil-plant relationships reveals that under certain conditions soils may be expected to form which are selenium-deficient. Such deficiency may be expected particularly in acid soils derived from igneous parent materials, and it may be aggravated in some soils by excessive leaching caused by irrigation. Prediction of selenium-deficiency conditions for livestock from soil data is complicated by several factors, however. The availability of soil selenium is affected by the chemical form in which it exists, as well as by the presence or absence of certain interfering factors, such as sulphate. In addition, variances exist in the extent to which different plant species can absorb selenium from the soil at physiological levels or less. These variations are much less spectacular than those which exist at the toxic end of the selenium spectrum, involving the so-called "accumulator" plants, but their effects may be no less damaging to animal health.

Finally, some means have been demonstrated for overcoming selenium deficiency by either pasture top-dressing or soil amendment. Available data indicate that, at best, soil treatment is an inefficient way of providing selenium in terms of the amounts required by animals. Moreover, the dangers of selenium toxicity, coupled with the variations in selenium availability and uptake from various kinds of soil by the many different species of forage plants, suggest caution in the use of these methods of alleviating selenium deficiencies among animals.

REFERENCES CITED

Allaway, W. H., 1968a, Control of the environmental levels of selenium. Proc. 2d ann. conf. on trace substances in environmental health: Columbia, Univ. Missouri, p. 181–206.

—— 1968b, The chemistry of selenium: Proc. Semi-Annual Meeting, Am. Feed Manuf. Assoc., v. 126, p. 355–361.

Allaway, W. H., and Hodgson, J. F., 1964, Selenium in forages as related to the geographic distribution of muscular dystrophy in livestock: Jour. Animal Sci., v. 23, p. 271–277.

Allaway, W. H., Moore, D. P., Oldfield, J. E., and Muth, O. H., 1966, Movement of physiological levels of selenium from soils, through plants to animals: Jour. Nutrition, v. 88, p. 414–418.

Beath, O. A., Draize, J. H., and Eppson, H. F., 1932, Three poisonous vetches: Wyoming Agric. Exp. Stn. Bull. 189, 23 p.

Beath, O. A., Draize, J. H., and Gilbert, C. S., 1934, Plants poisonous to livestock: Wyoming Agr. Exp. Stn. Bull. 200, 84 p.

Beeson, K. C., 1961, Occurrence and significance of selenium in plants, *in* Selenium in agriculture: U.S. Dept. Agric. Handb. 200, p. 34–40.

Blaxter, K. L., Brown, F., and MacDonald, A. M., 1953, The nutrition of the young Ayrshire calf. 12. Factors affecting the tocopherol reserves, muscle composition and muscle histology of four-day-old calves: British Jour. Nutrition, v. 7, p. 105–123.

Cannon, Helen L., 1969, Trace element excesses and deficiencies in some geochemical provinces of the United States, *in* Trace substances in environmental health, III: Columbia, Univ. Missouri, p. 21–43.

Carter, D. L., Brown, M. J., Allaway, W. H., and Cary, E. E., 1968, Selenium content of forage and hay crops in the Pacific Northwest: Agronomy Jour., v. 60, p. 532–534.

Cary, E. E., Wieczorek, G. A., and Allaway, W. H., 1967, Reactions of selenite-Se added to soils that produce low-Se forages: Soil Sci. Soc. America Proc., v. 31, p. 21–26.

Cousins, F. B., and Cairney, I. M., 1961, Some aspects of selenium metabolism in sheep: Australian Jour. Agric. Research, v. 12, p. 927–942.

Davies, E. B., and Watkinson, J. H., 1966, Uptake of native and applied selenium by pasture species. I. Uptake of Se by browntop, ryegrass, cocks foot and white clover from Atiamuri sand: New Zealand Jour. Agric. Research, v. 9, p. 317–327.

Davies, E. B., and Watkinson, J. H., 1966, Uptake of native and applied selenium by pasture species. II. Effect of sulfate and soil type on uptake by clover: New Zealand Jour. Agric. Research, v. 9, p. 641–652.

Ehlig, C. F., Allaway, W. H., Cary, E. E., and Kubota, Joe, 1968, Differences among plant species in selenium accumulation from soils low in available selenium: Agronomy Jour., v. 60, p. 43–47.

Fleming, G. A., and Walsh, T., 1957, Selenium occurrence in certain Irish soils and its toxic effect upon animals: Royal Irish Acad. Proc. 58, Sec. b, p. 151–165.

Frost, D. V., 1965, Selenium and poultry. An exercise in nutrition toxicology which involves arsenic: Worlds Poultry Sci. Jour., v. 21, p. 139–156.

Ganther, H. E., 1965, The fate of selenium in animals: World Rev. Nutrition & Dietetics, v. 5, 5:338–366.

Ganther, H. E., and Baumann, C. A., 1962, Selenium metabolism. II. Modifying effects of sulfate: Jour. Nutrition, v. 77, p. 408–414.

Gardiner, M. R., 1962, White muscle disease (nutritional muscular dystrophy) of sheep in Western Australia: Australian Vet. Jour., v. 38, p. 387–391.

—— 1969, Selenium in animal nutrition: Outlook Agric., v. 6, p. 19–28.

Gardiner, M. R., and Gorman, R. C., 1963, Further observations on plant selenium levels in Western Australia: Australian Jour. Exp. Agric. and Animal Husb., v. 3, p. 284–289.

Grant, A. B., 1965, Pasture top-dressing with selenium: New Zealand Jour. Agric. Research, v. 8, p. 681–690.

Hamilton, J. W., and Beath, O. A., 1963, Uptake of available selenium by certain range plants: Jour. Range Manage., v. 16, p. 261–264.

Hurd-Karrer, A. M., 1935, Factors affecting absorption of Se from soil by plants: Jour. Agric. Research, v. 50, p. 413–427.

Hurd-Karrer, A. M., and Kennedy, M. H., 1936, Inhibiting effect of sulphur in selenized soil on toxicity of wheat to rats: Jour. Agric. Research, v. 52, p. 933–942.

Kubota, J., Allaway, W. H., Carter, D. L., Cary, E. E., and Lazar, V. A., 1967, Selenium in crops in the United States in relation to selenium-responsive diseases of animals: Agric. and Food Chem., v. 15, p. 448–453.

Lakin, H. W., 1961, Geochemistry of selenium in relation to agriculture, *in* Selenium in agriculture: Agric. Handb. 200, U.S. Dept. Agric. p. 3–12.

Lakin, H. W., and Davidson, D. F., 1967, The relation of the geochemistry of selenium to its occurrence in soils, *in* Symposium: Selenium in biomedicine: Westport, Conn., AVI Pub. Co., p. 27–56.

Leggett, J. E., and Epstein, E., 1956, Kinetics of sulfate absorption by barley roots: Plant Physiol., v. 31, p. 222–226.

McCoy, K.E.M., and Weswig, P. H., 1969, Some selenium responses in the rat not related to vitamin E: Jour. Nutrition, v. 98, p. 383–389.

Moxon, A. L., Olson, O. E., and Searight, W. V., 1950, Selenium in rocks, soils and plants: Tech. Bull. 2, South Dakota Agr. Exp. Sta., 93 pp.

Muth, O. H., 1955, White muscle disease (myopathy) in lambs and calves. I. Occurrence and nature of the disease under Oregon conditions: Jour. Am. Vet. Med. Assoc., v. 126, p. 355–361.

Muth, O. H., 1963, White muscle disease, a selenium-responsive myopathy: Jour. Am. Vet. Med. Assoc., v. 142, p. 272–277.

Muth, O. H., and Allaway, W. H., 1963, The relationship of white muscle disease to the distribution of naturally-occurring selenium: Jour. Am. Vet. Med. Assoc., v. 142, p. 1379–1384.

Muth, O. H., Oldfield, J. E., Remmert, L. F., and Schubert, J. R., 1958, Effects of selenium and vitamin E on white muscle disease: Science, v. 128, p. 1090.

Patterson, E. L., Milstrey, R., and Stokstad, E.L.R., 1957, Effect of selenium in preventing exudative diathesis in chicks: Soc. Exp. Biol. & Med. Proc., v. 95, p. 617–620.

Peterson, P. J., and Butler, G. W., 1962, The uptake and assimilation of selenite by higher plants: Australian Jour. Biol. Sci., v. 15, p. 126–146.

Peterson, P. J., and Spedding, D. J., 1963, The excretion by sheep of selenium incorporated into red clover (*Trifolium pratense L.*): The chemical nature of the excreted selenium and its uptake by three plant species: New Zealand Jour. Agric. Research, v. 6, p. 18–23.

Ravikovitch, S., and Margolin, M., 1957, Selenium in soils and plants: Israel Agric. Exp. Stn. Rehovot. Series 145-E 7, p. 41–52.

Roughan, P. G., 1965, A succinoxidase inhibitor associated with fresh, leguminous pastures: New Zealand Jour. Agric. Research, v. 8, p. 607–612.

Schwarz, K., 1961, Nutritional significance of selenium (Factor 3): Federation Proc. 20, p. 665.

Schwarz, K., and Foltz, C. M., 1957, Selenium as an integral part of Factor 3 against dietary necrotic liver degeneration: Jour. Am. Chem. Soc., v. 79, p. 3292–3293.

Sharman, G.A.M., 1960, Selenium in animal health: Nutr. Soc. Proc., v. 19, p. 169–176.

Shrift, A., 1961, Biochemical interrelations between selenium and sulphur in plants and microorganisms: Federation Proc., v. 20, no. 2, p. 1, p. 695–702.

Taboury, M. F., and Coudray-Viau, O., 1939, Effect de la fixation du selenium par quelques cruciferes sur les rapports quantitatifs de certains elements dans ces vegetaux: Acad. Sciences Comptes. Rendus, v. 209, p. 121–123.

Thompson, J. N., and Scott, M. L., 1968, Selenium deficiency in chicks and quail: Cornell Conf. for Feed Manuf. Proc., p. 130–136.

Trelease, S. F., and Beath, O. A., 1949, Selenium. Its geological occurrence and its biological effects in relation to botany, chemistry, agricultural nutrition and medicine: Burlington, Vermont, Champlain Printers, 292 p.

Whanger, P. D., Muth, O. H., Oldfield, J. E., and Weswig, P. H., 1969, Influence of sulfur on incidence of white muscle disease in lambs: Jour. Nutrition, v. 97, p. 553–562.

Williams, K. G., and Byers, H. G., 1935, Occurrence of selenium in the Colorado River and some of its tributaries: Ind. Eng. Chem. (Anal. Ed.), v. 7, p. 431–432.

Young, S., and Keeler, R., 1962, Nutritional muscular dystrophy in lambs—the effect of muscular activity on the symmetrical distribution of lesions: Am. Jour. Vet. Research, v. 23, p. 966–971.

Manuscript Received by The Society June 9, 1971

Published as Special Paper 332, Oregon Agricultural Experiment Station

Published in The Geological Society of America Bulletin, January, 1972.

PRINTED IN U.S.A.

The Geological Society of America, Inc.
Special Paper 140, 1972

Distribution of Trace Elements in the Environment and the Occurrence of Heart Disease in Georgia

Hansford T. Shacklette
U.S. Geological Survey, Denver, Colorado 80225
Herbert I. Sauer
Environmental Health Surveillance and Research Center, Columbia, Missouri 65201
Alfred T. Miesch
U.S. Geological Survey, Denver, Colorado 80225

ABSTRACT

The concentrations of certain chemical elements in native plants, garden vegetables, and soils were studied in two areas of Georgia, each made up of nine counties, that have greatly different heart disease mortality rates. The soils of the two areas were found to be geochemically distinct. The greater amounts of trace elements in soils occur in the counties that have the lower death rates, but the abundances of trace elements in trees and vegetables do not correspond closely to the abundances in the soils. The trace elements in soils, however, may have entered the human food chain in water, in other food plants, and in meat and milk that were not sampled in this study. If geochemical differences between the soils of the high-death-rate area and the low-death-rate area do, in fact, have a causal relationship to death from cardiovascular diseases, the cause would appear to be a deficiency, rather than an excess, of the elements that were studied.

INTRODUCTION

A cooperative study was conducted in 1963–1965 by the U.S. Geological Survey and the Heart Disease and Stroke Control Program, U.S. Public Health Service, of two groups of contiguous or nearby counties known to have greatly different cardiovascular mortality rates. This study was described in detail by Shacklette and others (1970). One group of nine counties is in central and south-central Georgia, and counties of this group have mortality rates that are roughly double, or more than double, the rates of nine counties of the other group which is located in northern Georgia. All the high-rate counties, but one, lie entirely within the Coastal Plain region, whereas the low-rate counties are in the Blue Ridge, the Valley and Ridge, and the upper part of the Piedmont provinces of the Appalachian Highlands region (Fig. 1). The striking spatial correspondence of distinct death-rate areas and physiographic regions in Georgia suggested that some influence of the physical environment, possibly the chemical elements in natural materials, may have contributed to the difference in rates of the two groups of counties. This hypothesis was strengthened by known differences in rocks and soils of the two groups that would contribute to geochemical differences.

CARDIOVASCULAR MORTALITY RATES

Death rates for the cardiovascular diseases include those for coronary heart disease, stroke, hypertensive diseases, and other diseases of the

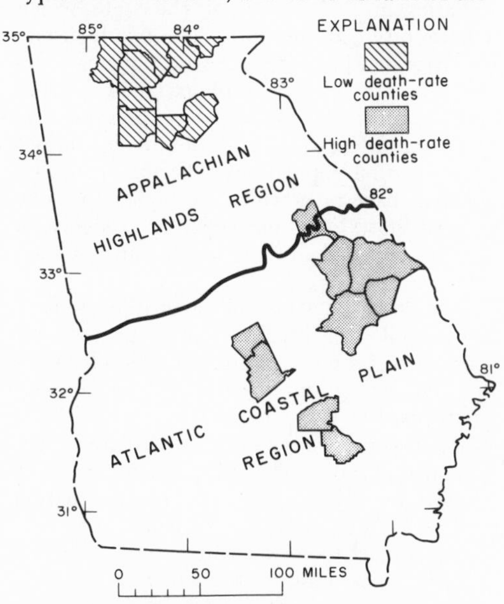

Figure 1. Physiographic regions of Georgia, and groups of counties having high and low rates of death due to cardiovascular diseases.

heart and blood vessels. Rates were computed for the state by usual county of residence, utilizing all deaths for the period 1950–1959, inclusive. Standard vital statistics techniques were used in computing rates, which are expressed as average annual death rates per 100,000 population at risk, along with several refinements to meet the specific needs of this type of ecological study.

The age-sex group of greatest epidemiological concern is that of middle-aged white males, which has been defined broadly as white males of age 35 to 74. Rates were computed for this age group, using the average of the 1950 and 1960 censuses as the population at risk, and have been adjusted by the direct method by 10-yr age groups to the total United States population of that age in 1950. Differences in death rates, therefore, are not due to differences in the age, sex, or race composition of the populations of the various counties.

Nine contiguous low-rate counties, in which the death rate for white males age 35 to 74 ranged from 560 to 682, were chosen for this study. Three other counties had rates equally low, but these counties had very small populations of middle-aged white males; therefore, they were excluded from this study. Of 18 counties that could be classified as "high rate," with death rates from 1,151 to 1,446, nine were chosen for the study because they are rural counties in the section of the state which consistently had high rates. The two high-rate counties in which the cities of Savannah and Augusta are located were excluded because local geochemical factors were presumed to have less effect on metropolitan populations than on rural populations. The nine high-rate counties have rates which are higher than the United States rate, and which are roughly 90 percent higher than those for the nine low-rate counties.

The death rates for "all noncardiovascular" causes follow a pattern similar to that for cardiovascular diseases, and the all-causes rates for the two groups of counties show similar contrasts. For white females age 35 to 74 the pattern of rates was similar to that for males, but because of fewer deaths among white females in this age group, chance fluctuation will be higher. Although nonwhite rates generally parallel those for whites, the number of nonwhites in most of the northern Georgia counties is too small to provide a basis for calculating meaningful rates.

These contrasts in rates are, in general, not due to random error and, thus far, show no evidence of being due to methods of data collection or classification: we have made extensive search for such evidence.

In rural counties with small populations, it is reasonable to expect fluctuations in death rates, particularly for such a short period of time as 3 yrs. Even so, in the counties selected on the basis of their 1950–1959 rates, the cardiovascular death rates were substantially higher in each of the nine high-rate counties than in any of the low-rate counties for 1959–1961 (Table 1). This generalization applies as well for deaths from all causes as for cardiovascular deaths.

In comparison with the United States as a whole, these areas may properly be classified as "low" and "high." Specifically, of the 509 state economic areas of the United States, 8 percent had cardiovascular diseases rates lower than the median of these nine Georgia low-rate counties, and only 1 percent had rates higher than the median of the nine high-rate counties in this study. There is an incentive, therefore,

TABLE 1. RATES OF DEATH FROM CARDIOVASCULAR-RENAL DISEASES AND FROM ALL CAUSES, WHITE MALES, AGE 35-74, IN SELECTED COUNTIES OF GEORGIA, 1959-1961*

	Average annual rates of death	
	Cardiovascular-renal diseases†	All causes
Nine low-rate counties		
Cherokee	828.6	1,358.1
Fannin	757.2	1,334.3
Forsyth	740.1	1,286.0
Gilmer	701.9	1,228.7
Hall	867.9	1,463.1
Murray	643.7	1,463.3
Pickens	650.0	1,355.1
Towns	451.9	1,027.2
Union	607.1	1,168.0
Nine high-rate counties		
Bacon	1,494.0	2,486.2
Bleckley	922.8	1,576.2
Burke	982.7	1,775.3
Dodge	1,398.1	2,105.7
Emanuel	1,146.5	1,845.6
Jeff Davis	1,096.9	1,632.2
Jefferson	1,147.7	1,794.1
Jenkins	1,194.7	1,715.7
Warren	1,137.1	1,948.7

* *Average annual death rates per 100,000 population, age adjusted by 10-yr age groups by the direct method to the entire United States population age 35-74 in 1950. Death tabulated by National Center for Health Statistics by county of usual residence.*

† *Diseases included in these data are classified by code numbers 330-334, 400-468, and 592-594, World Health Organization (1957).*

to search for and test hypotheses regarding factors that may be responsible for these differences in death rates.

Forests occupy a substantial part, ranging from 45 to 81 percent, of all these counties, but the low-rate counties in the northern part of the state have a higher percentage of their area classified as forests (Georgia Business Research, 1963). Most counties in each group had decreases in population in the period 1950–1960: the high-rate counties have the larger decrease. The high-rate counties also have larger farms and thus are less densely populated. Both groups of counties are clearly nonmetropolitan and are rather sparsely populated. These differences between the two groups of counties illustrate the many variables that may be considered for further study.

GEOCHEMICAL CHARACTERIZATION AND SAMPLING PLAN FOR THE AREAS

The relation of the two areas of contrasting rates of heart disease mortality to the occurrence of rock and soil types can be summarized by stating that the high-mortality counties have soils that are derived from the highly weathered sedimentary deposits of the coastal plains and, therefore, are depleted of many chemical elements. The low-mortality counties, in contrast, have soils that originated from a great variety of rock types from which weathering continuously provides a fresh supply of chemical elements to the soils.

Within each of the two groups of counties, 30 sites were selected for sampling native plants (trees and shrubs) and uncultivated soils, and 30 sites were chosen for sampling vegetables and garden soils, a total of 120 sample sites in the two areas. Tree samples were analyzed in order to obtain some measure of availability of soil elements to deep-rooted plants, and vegetables were sampled because of their direct entry into the human food chain. Black-eyed peas, cabbage, corn, green beans, lima beans, and tomatoes were found to occur most frequently in gardens of both areas. Before analyses were performed, the vegetables were prepared in the same manner as for table use, then oven dried and burned to ash. Tree samples were separated into stems and leaves which were analyzed separately. The plow-zone soil only was sampled in gardens, whereas forest soils were divided into A-, B-, and C-horizon samples.

CHEMICAL ANALYSES OF SOILS AND PLANTS

All samples were analyzed, by emission spectroscopy and other methods, for 30 elements, and the results were evaluated by statistical methods (Shacklette and others, 1970). Soils from the low-death-rate counties were found to contain significantly larger concentrations of aluminum, barium, calcium, chromium, copper, iron, potassium, magnesium, manganese, niobium, phosphorus, titanium, and vanadium. Differences in boron, cobalt, lanthanum, nickel, lead, scandium, strontium, yttrium, and ytterbium were not significant. Only zirconium occurred in significantly larger concentrations in the high-death-rate counties. The differences in composition of soils from the two areas were so pronounced that they could have been determined by sampling only one of the three soil horizons. The levels of element concentration in forest soils and garden soils were very similar; the effects, if present, of fertilizing and cultivating the gardens could not be detected by our analyses.

The differences in elemental composition of the soils from the two areas were not reflected in the compositions of most of the vegetables, with the possible exception of cabbage and green beans. Cabbages from the low-death-rate area, like the soils, tend to contain larger concentrations of aluminum, chromium, iron, nickel, and titanium. The concentrations of several elements in green beans similarly appear to reflect the compositional differences in soils between the two areas, but those in the other vegetables do not. Within both the low- and high-death-rate areas, concentration in a particular garden soil and the concentrations in vegetables grown on this soil failed to indicate a relationship between soil and vegetable compositions.

Comparisons of the element content of the three horizons of uncultivated soils and of eight species of trees from the two death-rate areas indicate that concentrations of most elements in both soils and trees are higher in the low-death-rate area. Trees, therefore, may be more effective than vegetables in reflecting the chemical nature of the soil on which they grow. However, as with vegetables, no general relation was found between the compositions of a tree and the soil on which it grew within either of the two areas.

Caution should be used in making generalizations of plant-soil relations based on the data of this study. The concentrations of the elements that were studied in Georgia soils are all believed to be within the "normal" range. The fact is well known that some plants, if growing on soils that have highly anomalous amounts of certain elements, contain greater than normal amounts of these elements. The enrichment of metals in plants often has been described from analyses of vegetation that grew over mineral deposits.

TRACE ELEMENTS IN WATER

Water as a source of trace elements in the human diet was definitely recognized by us, but the resources and time required for evaluating the chemical composition of waters were not available for this study. In order to properly sample water to determine its possible effects on human health, the sources of the water that was consumed by the population at risk must be known; this information is not available for the two areas of this study. Domestic water used by populations in these areas most likely was supplied from individual sources for each rural family or small town. These sources doubtless were commonly used at least in the early years of individuals in the age group 35 to 74, because municipal water supplies for most small towns and rural areas were introduced only recently, if at all.

Local water sources include cisterns for holding rainwater, shallow wells, springs, and surface water from streams, ponds, and lakes, whereas municipal supplies generally are from either surface waters or deep wells. Because the chemical quality of water from different sources within an area may differ greatly, definite statements regarding the chemical elements in water consumed by inhabitants of an area require support by carefully planned programs of sampling and analysis. Nevertheless, some information from the literature may provide useful suggestions or generalizations, and also point out the inadequacy of our knowledge concerning the chemical composition of potable waters in the two death-rate areas.

Reports of the composition in trace elements of the waters that could have been consumed by the population at risk in this geohealth study are entirely inadequate for correlations with epidemiological data. Most reports of water analysis give only the concentrations of major elements that are generally recognized to affect the quality of water for domestic, agricultural, and industrial uses. In the report of Kopp and Kroner (undated) on trace metals in waters of the United States, only nine surveillance system sampling points are shown in the entire Southeast Basin (including all, or parts, of Virginia, North Carolina, South Carolina, Georgia, Florida, Alabama, and Mississippi); none of these sampling points falls in, or near, either of the two death-rate groups of Georgia counties. In that report, Kopp and Kroner stated (Appendix C-1),

> Composite samples from the [Southeast] basin analyzed during the time period involved [Oct. 1, 1962-Sept. 30, 1967] totaled 91. All elements included in the spectrographic program were observed on at least one occasion. Cadmium, beryllium, cobalt and vanadium were the lesser observed elements, occurring with a frequency of only 1.1%. Only barium occurred with a frequency of 100%; five other elements were observed at measurable levels in more than 94% of all samples. The basin's mean value for both iron and aluminum exceeded the national averages by a factor of two. All other elements were either equal to, or below, national averages.

LeGrand (1967, p. 8) wrote,

> In comparison with ground water in widely scattered regions of the world, the water in the Piedmont and Blue Ridge provinces ranks among the best in chemical quality. Most of the water is low in total dissolved solids and is generally soft, but some is moderately hard. Iron in water is the most common complaint. As little as 0.4 ppm (parts per million) will cause a red stain on plumbing fixtures. About 5 of every 10 wells yield water with less than 0.3 ppm of iron. About 4 of 10 wells yield water with just enough iron to cause a slight stain, and about 1 of 10 wells yields water that has considerable iron. . . . Most of the water is satisfactory for use without any type of treatment.

Other trace elements in water were not discussed by LeGrand.

Chemical characteristics of soils can affect the concentration of elements not only in surface waters, but also in ground waters. With special reference to the Appalachian Highlands region, LeGrand (1967, p. 9–10) stated,

> In general, wells are more productive and tend to have a more stable year-round yield where there is a thick mantle of soil than where bare rock crops out. . . . Where there is a good soil cover, the water table generally lies in it; therefore, the storage capacity in the vicinity is much greater than where bare rock is exposed and where the only water in storage is in the rock fractures that might be

quickly drained. . . . There is a tendency for rocks underlying a light-colored soil to yield water that is low in dissolved mineral matter and is soft. On the other hand, rocks underlying darker soils (dark red, brown, and yellow) tend to yield water that is slightly hard, or hard, and that may contain objectionable amounts of iron.

The well logs of the Coastal Plain of Georgia were discussed by Herrick (1961), who stated (p. 3),

> The strata of Tertiary age are the most important sources of ground water in the Coastal Plain as a whole, and the geologically older beds of Cretaceous age are important as water-bearing formations only along the upper limits of the Coastal Plain, immediately downdip from the Fall Line.

Of the well logs presented, 28 were of wells drilled in the high-death-rate counties of this study during the period 1888 to 1959; the potential water-bearing zones of the wells were in rock types as follows: 14 in sandstone, 8 in limestone, and 6 in both sandstone and limestone. Although water from limestone is expected to contain more total dissolved solids (expressed as hardness) than water from sandstone, the well logs discussed by Herrick suggest that there is great local variation in the quality of water from deep wells in the high-death-rate counties. The trace-element content of water may be an important factor in human and animal health, and the concentration of these elements does not necessarily correlate with degree of hardness. These observations point out the fact that in the absence of carefully controlled data, caution is necessary in making regional generalizations of water chemistry in relation to health problems.

TRACE ELEMENTS THAT AFFECT CARDIOVASCULAR FUNCTION

Masironi (1969) listed the trace elements that allegedly have beneficial effects on cardiovascular function as follows: manganese, chromium, vanadium, cobalt, zinc, fluorine, selenium, silicon, and copper. Of these elements, we found manganese, chromium, vanadium, and copper to be more highly concentrated in soils from the low-death-rate counties. Cobalt was somewhat more concentrated in soils from these counties, but differences in concentrations between the two groups of counties were not significant. Analyses are not available for fluorine, selenium, and silicon in the soils. Silicon is seldom a limiting factor in plant and animal growth because it is a major constituent of most soils. Elements allegedly having harmful effects on cardiovascular function are cobalt (when injected), fluorine (in large doses), selenium, copper, cadmium, and arsenic (in large doses). In view of Masironi's summary, the low cardiovascular death rate in northern Georgia may possibly be related to the abundance of beneficial trace elements in the soils. We did not find excess concentrations of harmful elements in the soils from counties with higher death rates in central and south-central Georgia. The possible importance of cadmium, fluorine, and selenium in these soils, however, remains unknown.

SUMMARY AND CONCLUSION

In summary, this study indicates that although the geochemistry of soils in the two death-rate areas of Georgia is very different, the difference between the two areas in the level of elements present in vegetables appears to be so slight as to be unlikely to contribute appreciably to the observed difference in death rates in middle-aged humans. The study shows that garden vegetables do not clearly reflect the chemical compositions of the soils on which the vegetables grew. The chemicals in soils, however, may enter the human food chain in water, in food plants that were not sampled in this study, and in meat and milk from animals that have fed on cultivated forage plants and native vegetation.

If geochemical differences between the soils of the two areas do, in fact, have a causal relationship to death from cardiovascular diseases, the cause would appear to be a deficiency, rather than an excess, of the elements that were studied.

REFERENCES CITED

Georgia Business Research, 1963, Georgia statistical abstract: Athens, Georgia Univ., 418 p.

Herrick, S. M., 1961, Well logs of the Coastal Plain of Georgia: Georgia Geol. Survey Bull. 70, 462 p.

Kopp, J. F., and Kroner, R. C. [undated], Trace metals in waters of the United States—A five-year summary of trace metals in rivers and lakes of the United States (Oct. 1, 1962-Sept. 30, 1967): Cincinnati, Ohio, U.S. Dept. of Interior, Federal Water Pollution Control Administration, 29 p. + append.

LeGrand, H. E., 1967, Ground water of the Piedmont and Blue Ridge provinces in the Southeastern States: U.S. Geol. Survey Circ. 538, 11 p.

Masironi, Roberto, 1969, Trace elements and cardiovascular diseases: Geneva, World Health Organization Bull., v. 40, p. 305–312.

Shacklette, H. T., Sauer, H. I., and Miesch, A. T., 1970, Geochemical environments and cardiovascular mortality rates in Georgia: U.S. Geol. Survey Prof. Paper 574-C, 39 p.

World Health Organization, 1957, Manual of the international statistical classification of diseases, injuries and causes of death, 7th revision: Geneva, World Health Organization, v. 1, 393 p.

Manuscript Received by the Society June 9, 1971

Publication Authorized by the Director, U.S. Geological Survey, Washington, D.C.

Published in The Geological Society of America Bulletin, April, 1972.

PRINTED IN U.S.A.

Index